gaz regan's
Annual Manual
for Bartenders

2011

D1563428

gaz regan's
Annual Manual
for Bartenders
2011

gaz regan

MIXELLANY

mixellany limited

Copyright © 2011 by Gary Regan.

Photo credits: Vanessa Bahmani 343; Leo Borovsky/Lush Life 165; Jared Brown cover photo, 99, 103, 108, 109, 119, 120, 129, 133, 135, 137, 139, 141; Starchefs 208

Illustration credit: Stuffy Schmitt 22

Mixellany books may be purchased for educational, business, or sales promotional use. For information, please write to Mixellany Limited, 3 Eyford Cottages, Upper Slaughter, Cheltenham, Gloucestershire GL54 2JL United Kingdom. or email jared@mixellany.com

First edition

ISBN 13: 978-1-907434-19-8

British Library Cataloguing in Publication Data.
A catalogue record for this book is available from the British Library.

This book is dedicated
to bartenders everywhere.

gaz regan's **ANNUAL MANUAL FOR BARTENDERS** 2011

ACKNOWLEDGMENTS

Martha Schueneman, my trusty editor, brought lots to this project. Lots. Thanks Martha. Thanks also to Jared Brown and Anistatia Miller for being fabulous publishers, and good friends. And thanks to each and every person mentioned in this book, and everyone who contributed their thoughts, recipes, and philosophies. I'm one of the happiest people I know, and bartenders all over the world help me stay that way. Ta Muchly.

TABLE OF CONTENTS

INTRODUCTION

Welcome to the first *Annual Manual for Bartenders*. I'm very excited about this concept—it's something that I've been batting around in my head for the past few years. More than anything, this thing was born because I felt that it would be a good idea to set down in writing who has been doing what in the realm of the bartender during the first decade of the 21st century. This way, bartenders in the 22nd century will be able to say, "God bless Jamie Boudreau for teaching us about slapping herbs," and "Where would we be today if Eben Freeman hadn't taught the world about fat washing." Stuff like that there.

Books, in my experience, never end up being true to the original concept, and this one's a good example. I started adding bits, thinking of new chapters, and generally trying to put together something that's aimed directly at working bartenders—something that I don't believe has been done before—and trying to make it a book that's truly useful. Did I succeed? Your call. It's your round, too, I think ...

Part 1

A Serialized Autobiography: My First 17 Years on God's Green Earth

I've been writing my autobiography since 2002 and I've never been happy with the way it ends. I can't seem to tie it up neatly. Perhaps there's something that lies ahead for me, and I won't be able to finish this darned thing until it happens. Anyway, since the *Annual Manual* is going to be a series, I thought that I'd bring you one or two chapters in each edition, and we'll see how that works out.

Here, then, is the introduction to my autobiography along with the first two chapters, bringing you from the day I was born through the time I'm around 17 years old. I've had a fabulous life, and I'd like to share everything– or almost everything–with you.

An Autobiography, by gaz regan

Introduction

I've spent my entire life in and around bars and booze, and like everyone else who lives this lifestyle, I've gone through many ups and many downs along the way. I know that everyone here on God's green earth goes through ups and downs in life, and I'm not saying that mine have been greater than anyone else's, but if you're a boozer, and chances are that, since you're reading this book, you probably enjoy a drink or two, then lots of your ups and downs are directly involved with drinks or drinking. One minute you're at a fabulous cocktail party in Hollywood meeting celebrities you've dreamed of meeting, and the next minute you're homeless and trying to scrounge enough scratch to buy a pint of cheap vodka. I've never been in either of those situations (thank God on both accounts), but booze has certainly been a common thread in my life. Booze has brought me lots of high points, and it's resulted in quite a few pretty drastic lows, too. I wouldn't change one second of my life, and here I am in 2011, 59 years old and the happiest I've ever been. I've had a damned interesting ride, and I'm determined to keep it going for another forty years or more, too. I'm aiming to live until I'm 100. Distillers take note: Start laying some barrels of whiskey down for me, please.

I've met my fair share of characters during my nigh-on six decades in the booze biz. Most of them have just been larger-than-life civilians and bartender types, but I've also had brushes with a few rich-and-famous people, too. The one person I never expected to bump into in a barroom, though, has been in every single joint I worked at or drank in, but I didn't meet Her until 2004. That was the year I bumped into God. She was hiding in plain sight, sitting at the end of the bar sipping a Dry Gin Martini. I walked over and started a conversation. She's good at barroom banter, is God. Stick around for future installations and I'll introduce you, but we've got some serious drinking to do before we meet Her.

Grab you coat, grab your hat, and grab your wallet. The bars are open, and we're expected.

Chapter 1

Bernard John Regan Becomes a Dad

Here's a map of Lancashire so you'll have a bit of a clue where the towns in the following story are located. Lancashire sits right above Wales on the left coast of England, in case you weren't sure (and Wales is the "pig's head" that juts out into the Irish Sea). Map illustrated by Stuffy Schmitt.

At two o'clock in the A.M. on the eighteenth of September, 1951, Bernard John Regan, landlord of the Horse and Jockey, a pub on Well'I'Th' Lane, Rochdale, Lancashire, England, became my father. He was in a police station at the time. Dad wasn't in trouble with the law, though, he just needed someone to talk to. He was worried about his wife, Vi Regan, the woman I'd call Mum once I could get my tongue around it. Vi had been in labor for a full seven days before I made my appearance, you see, and things were looking a wee bit grim for the both of us. Poor Bernard was at his wit's end.

When he told me this story, about 14 years later, Dad went on to explain that a policeman had taken him to the hospital that night, and when he found out that I'd finally decided to make my way toward that light at the end of the tunnel, and that Mum and I were both just fine and dandy, he had gone back to the pub, knocking on friends' doors in and around Well'I'Th' Lane as he strolled, and he'd invited all and sundry down to the pub to celebrate with pints of free ale. "And I think that, at some point down the road," he told me, "you might want to think about paying for at least half the bar bill."

Left: Bernard at the Horse & Jockey.
Right: Vi pulls a pint at the Horse & Jockey.

My future, it seems, was set in stone within hours of my birth. I was fated to follow in Bernard's footsteps, and like him, I've been a professional boozer all my life.

My earliest memory goes back to when I was about three years old—I vividly remember standing on a chair playing with toys in the sink in the kitchen. But by this time we were living in a flat above my mother's dress shop in the Cleveleys end of Thornton-Cleveleys, a small middle-class seaside resort on the northwest coast of England, some fifty-odd miles away from the somewhat grimy industrial town of Rochdale where I'd been born. When I got to be about two years old, Vi had managed to persuade Bernard that it might be best to raise me outside of the pub game, and he'd reluctantly resigned his post at the Horse and Jockey and taken a job as a bar-cellarman—he worked behind the bar and he also looked after the real ale in the beer cellar—at the Cleveleys Hotel, a pub just down the road a piece from Vi's shop.

On reflection, Bernard gave up a lot in order to bring me up outside of the pub game. As landlord and landlady of the Horse and Jockey, he and Vi had lived in a flat above the pub, renting the building from a brewery and running the pub as their own business. He was his own boss. At the Cleveleys Hotel he was a hired hand, and although there's nothing wrong with being a hired hand, Bernard, as you'll see very shortly, was born to be a headliner, not an extra.

Vi's mother Mary Elizabeth Armstrong, aka Nan Armstrong, had lived with my parents since before I was born, and it seemed to work out pretty well. My parents were busy trying to dig themselves out from under their pretty humble beginnings, and Nan did all of the cooking and cleaning. She was a second mother to me, was Nan. She stood about five-two or -three and she had one of those well-girdled bodies that grandmothers of her generation wore well. Nan was a round little woman. She had a huge heart, the patience of a saint, and was just full of love. Nan was everything good that all boys say about their mothers and grandmothers. She was one of eleven kids brought up in a tiny house in Rochdale with their mother and father, but just 10 of them were actually siblings. The eleventh was the daughter of a cousin, born out of wedlock, and taken in by Nan's family to save the cousin from the shame of it all. Such was the way of that generation.

When Nan was 12 years old, she'd been put to work at a local cotton mill, not because her parents were horrible, but because they couldn't make ends meet. She went to school two or three days a week and worked at the mill two or three days, too. If she cleaned under the looms during her lunch break at the mill, she was rewarded with an extra thre'pence come Friday, and Nan told me that she did that pretty frequently so she could have a little spending money of her own. "I always ended up handing it over to Mum, though," she said. "They didn't have enough money to put food on the table most the time."

Nan, seen here at the cotton mill, is seated, on your right. Margaret, one of her sisters is standing on your left.

One of my favorite stories about Nan Armstrong took place when she resigned her post as the manager of a social club in Rochdale—this was before I was born—and the regulars had thrown some cash together and bought her a teapot that was shaped like a rooster. "I filled it with rum," Nan told me, "and I went round all the customers telling them they had to have a drink out of my cock." Nan loved her dirty jokes. And I still have that teapot.

Before we left Rochdale and the Horse and Jockey, I should probably note, I'd already downed a glass of Guinness. It had belonged to Bernard's mother, Nan Regan. Lots of grandmothers in the U.K. get called *Nan*; it's akin to the word *granny*, I guess. Anyway, the story as it was told to me was that Nan

Regan was babysitting me in the flat above the pub, and after leaving me alone for a couple of minutes, she returned to find that her nightcap had disappeared. The glass was empty, and Baby Gary was smiling large. Let the boozing begin.

Vi's dress shop was less than a mile from the Irish Sea, and I spent a somewhat idyllic childhood in Cleveleys playing on the beach—we called it "the sands"—and hanging out in the amusement arcades, wasting my spending money on one-armed-bandits and the Thre'penny Derby, a Wheel-of-Fortune-type of game that ate up your money at triple the speed of the slots.

I met my best friend, Bill Greenham, on our first day of school when we were both five years old, and three years later Bill and I met Stan Ogden, a lad who had just moved to Cleveleys from Oldham, another grimy town in the industrial northwestern part of England. The three of us are friends to this day, and although he's a relative newcomer, Bill and I treat Stan like we're all three on equal footing. Hell, these days we even let Barry Irvin, a guy we've known for only, oh, about 40 years, think he's one of the gang.

Nan's (cock) teapot.

Stan Ogden, Barry Irvin, Bill Greenham, and gaz, 1997.

Bill has three sisters and a brother, whereas I'm an only child—understandable after one's mother goes through a full seven days of labor—so I spent lots of my time at Bill's house when I was a kid. I'd sit quietly in the Greenhams' kitchen watching the family interact, bribing each other to do chores, arguing, helping each other, and generally learning how to act like a family.

When I was about 10 years old, Vi, Bernard, Nan, and I moved to a small modern house just a block away from the sea, though Vi still ran the shop, and she sub-let the flat to a friend. Shortly thereafter I graduated from junior school and spent my first year in high school at Fleetwood Grammar. Schools were divided in those days, and the academically inclined were sent to grammar schools whereas those who looked as though they were heading toward the trades attended "secondary modern" schools. It was a system that was very flawed.

I was the only boy from my junior high school who went on to attend Fleetwood Grammar, but that wasn't because I was the only boy who passed his exams. All the other boys who passed had opted to go to Baines Grammar School, you see, but Baines was an all-boys school. I was having none of that. "What's the point in going to school at all if there are no girls there?" I thought. I'd latched on to my very first girl-friend when I was five years old—Catherine Booth, if memory serves—and then there was Deanne Eastwood. She and I were an item for a couple of years when we were about nine or ten. I saw her knickers once in the gym when she was doing a somersault. They were dark blue.

I fell in love with a girl called Linda at Fleetwood Grammar. She didn't respond well to my advances, even when I offered to take her to a Rolling Stones concert in Blackpool, the "Atlantic City" of England's northwestern coast, and a town that lies just a few miles to the south of Cleveleys. "I already have tickets," she told me. Undeterred, since Linda was what we would have called back then "a smashing looking bird," I prevailed on Vi and Bernard to let me go to the concert on the off-chance that I'd bump into Linda, and perhaps she and I would make out on the beach afterwards, and perhaps she'd let me touch her breasts, then she'd start groping me and we'd end up … Gimme a break, wudya? I was 12.

Mum and Dad got me a ticket. They got tickets for themselves, too, so in 1964 I saw the Stones perform. Jagger's white shirt had a dirty collar. He wore green elephant-cord pants—very art-school, though he went to the London School of Economics, of course. The show was perfection. Vi loved it, but Bernard hated every second. And that made it even more perfect. I loved them both, but Vi and I shared this thing about Bernard that sort of said, "He just doesn't get it, but we do."

I never got anywhere with the Linda girl, and that was probably for the best since in the summer of 1964, Bernard managed to convince Vi that now I was at high school and faring quite well academically, it would be just fine to get back into the pub business. He was right, of course, but not in the way in which Vi had in mind. I'd gotten good grades in Latin at Fleetwood Grammar, and I fared well in French, English, and math, too, but my academic skills weren't to last. Pub life was about to take its toll on my school work. Being the son of a pub landlord and landlady when I was 12, going on 13, made quite an impression on me. My life behind bars was about to begin.

Before we moved to Bolton, yet another grimy, industrial town in Lancashire, to get back into the pub game, I figured it was time for me to have another drink. That Guinness had tasted quite good back when I was two or three years old, after all, but I was thinking that I might like to follow in Dad's footsteps now that I was becoming a man, so gin was the name of my next quaff. My first Gin Gimlet was given to me at one of Vi and Bernard's Saturday night parties during my first year of high school, though I can't remember who poured it for me. I do remember thinking that I must never forget this drink. I knew that I always wanted to remember what my first taste of hard liquor was all about. We didn't call it a Gin Gimlet back then. Only swank bars in London would have known it by name. It was a Gin and Lime, pure and simple, and come to think of it, if you go into most pubs in Lancashire in the twenty-first century, that's still how you'd order the drink if you wanted a mixture of gin and lime juice cordial. Anyway, my Gin and Lime went down real well and I danced the night away to tunes by the Beatles and the Searchers and Gerry and the Pacemakers. Bernard didn't play the Stones at his parties.

I got along well with both Vi and Bernard during the Cleveleys years, and it wasn't until I was in my twenties that I started having a bit of a hard time with my Dad, simply because his drinking got out of control. Although he never intentionally hurt my Mum—he certainly never hit her, and neither did he ever threaten her; Bernard was a very kind and gentle man—but he did make life a bit difficult for her at times. I'll go into this stuff in more detail in later episodes, but it's important that you know that Vi and Bernard were very nurturing parents. Both of them loved me unconditionally, and they made sure that I knew that, too.

Bernard was larger than life. He loved to be center stage. He loved people. He loved to party. And he loved to sing and perform at every opportunity. He'd burst into song at the drop of a hat at a party, and he was a very generous man, too. If you needed help to paint a wall, if you were looking for advice about this thing or that, or if you wanted a loan of a few pounds, Bernard was the man to see. If he had it, it was yours for the asking. Vi was generous, too, and she was kind and good-natured. For the most part, though, she kept in the background when Bernard was around. Nobody could compete with such a massive personality as his. In the dress shop, Vi was a little different. There she was the boss, and she was very much respected by her customers. She got a fabulous reputation by telling people stuff like, "No, that's a great dress, but it's not for you. I can't let you buy that one. I've got three new shipments coming in next week. Pop by on Thursday and we'll find you something."

"Be honest," she used to tell me, "and you'll have customers who come back for the rest of their lives."

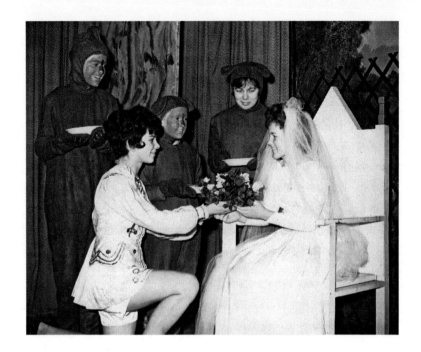

Here I am playing Baby Bear in a church production of the Goldilocks pantomime.

Dad had been in the Royal Air Force during WWII, and after the war was over he met Vi through her brother, Wilf Armstrong, a guy he worked with at some factory or other. Vi and Bernard fell in love and married, despite Bernard's mother's objections—Bernard was raised as a Catholic by Nan Regan, a woman I think of as being a Black-Belt Catholic, and Vi was a Sunday school teacher at a Congregationalist church. Neither of them was very religious, mind, though Vi was truly spiritual in a very special way. When good things happened she would look at me and say, "God is good." I paid no attention.

I went to church and Sunday school as a kid, and I loved being in the Christmas pantomimes that the church staged every year and going to the Saturday-night socials where we'd dance to local rock and roll bands, or we'd do some country dancing—barn dances and the like. I believed in Jesus, I think, but I didn't give it that much thought. I probably believed in him so that I could have a grand time at the socials. Religion certainly wasn't part of my life.

I didn't realize at the time that Congregationalists are, by and large, non-drinkers, so I was confused by the look on the Pastor's face when I told him that I wouldn't be coming to his church anymore because my parents were taking over a pub in Bolton. He was pretty gracious about it, shaking his head whilst smiling benevolently and wishing me well. I didn't look for a new church to attend once we got to Bolton. My social life shifted from the church to the pub, so I didn't need the Saturday-night socials any more. Pub life turned out to be a grand substitute for the church.

DIRTY TOM MCALEAR

"Perhaps the lowest of the Sydney-Town dives were the Boar's Head, where the principal attraction was a sexual exhibition in which a woman and a boar participated; the Goat and Compass and the Golden Rule, both owned by one Hell Haggerty, a ticket-of-leave man from Sydney; and the Fierce Grizzly, so called because a live female bear was kept chained beside the door. The Goat and Compass was the particular hang-out of a Sydney-Town character known as Dirty Tom McAlear, who for a few cents would eat or drink any sort of refuse offered to him."

The Barbary Coast: An Informal History of the San Francisco Underworld by Herbert Asbury, 1933.

gaz regan
Comes of Age

The Prince Rupert was a modern (for the 1960s) pub with a fair-sized wrap-around car park on a council estate in one of the roughest areas of Bolton. And Bolton was, and still can be, a pretty tough town. A council estate, lest you're not familiar with the term, is a neighborhood owned by the town council and rented to people who earn a low enough income to qualify—sort of like projects in the USA. Council estates can be rough and tumble, but that doesn't mean that there aren't lots of fabulous people there, as you're about to discover. Nevertheless, our move there from the mostly middle-class Cleveleys came as a pretty massive culture shock to me.

The kids at my new school—Bolton County Grammar School—made me fight with my fists, something that had never happened in Cleveleys. At school in Cleveleys, we just pushed each other around like big sissies till one of us said, "Oh yeah ... I'll get you tomorrow," and ran off to the safety of just about anywhere grown-ups could be found. I had a secret weapon, though, and it served me very well indeed. Little did my new Boltonian friends know that I had been a fairground boxer.

A couple of years before we moved to Bolton, I'd taken boxing lessons at a gym in Cleveleys that sat above a local pub called The Victoria. I was no good at the pugilistic arts at all.

My pal Bill Greenham had been the one who introduced me to the gym in the first place, and it was he who busted my nose at a boxing exhibition held at the Thornton-Cleveleys Gala, a week-long annual event that took place when the traveling fair hit town. There were three-legged races, sack races, egg-and-spoon races, carousels, dodge-'em cars, shooting ranges, candy floss (cotton candy), toffee apples, and there were coconuts and live goldfish to be won, too. I flushed more than my fair share of goldfish down the loo when I found them belly-up in the fish bowl three days after winning them.

The gala in question took place circa 1962. Bill and I would have been 10 or 11 years old. The gym set up a boxing ring on the playing fields next to the fairground, and they threw the two of us into the ring to the delight of our school friends and their parents, who stood around whooping and yelling, praying that they'd see one or the other of us get damaged. We didn't let them down, either. Bill quickly caught me with a right hook to the nose, and before we knew it blood was streaming down my face and the crowd was going wild, shouting and screaming. Finish him off, Bill, his second told him. Jeez, guys, we're just a couple of kids, you know.

It wasn't much fun getting a bloody nose that day, but it's been worth its weight in gold ever since. There aren't that many guys, after all, who can boast about being fairground boxers in their youth. Worth a busted snout any day of the week, that is. And the boxing lessons prepared me well for the following incident.

I was in the schoolyard at my new school in Bolton. It was my third day there and I was feeling my way around. There was a hierarchy at this school, and it was a kind of hierarchy I'd never encountered in Cleveleys. The toughest guy in each year was called cock of whatever grade he's in. Johnny Nichols, for instance, was the undisputed "cock-of-the-second-year." My new friends wanted, nay, *needed*, to find out on which step of the ladder I stood when it came to being tough.

"You couldn't beat Johnny Nichols," said one of the kids.

I looked at Johnny Nichols across the yard and conceded. No way I was going to take that fucker on.

"Pete Hampson could beat the shit out of you." The lads pointed at Hampson and I figured they were right.

The third guy they tried to pit me against, though, was a tall streak of bacon called Bill Bradbury. He looked pretty much like he was all skin and bone so I decided to take my chances. I crossed the yard and started to tell him he was a piece of shit until he either had to take a swing at me or risk looking like a complete asshole. He threw a right jab but I jumped back in time. It missed. We gathered ourselves, the rest of the guys formed a circle around us, and I took my boxer's stance, standing sideways to him to lessen his target area, and holding up my dukes in the prescribed manner. We danced around each other for awhile, the rest of the lads chanting "Do. Do. Do," as Boltoners were wont to chant whenever there was a fight going on. Before either of us actually landed a punch, though, Mr. Townshend, a stern teacher with a dark sadistic streak, barged through the crowd, grabbed us both by the hair right above our ears, and pulled hard. He dragged us inside where he proceeded to punish us with mandatory essays on the events leading up to the Battle of Hastings or some such nonsense and threats of the cane if we ever got caught fighting again. Face was saved all around, Bill Bradbury and I became pals, and the rest of the kids, who knew full well that Bill's lack of body meat didn't say a thing about how tough he was, more or less left me alone from then on. I'd had a go at Bradbury and I knew how to stand like a boxer. That seemed to be good enough for them.

I soon made friends with Johnny Nichols, first for insurance, but soon because he was the coolest kid at school. He was an exceptionally clever lad. Probably a genius, I think. And Johnny Nichols got into drugs when we were about 15. He ended up leaving school—or was he expelled?—becoming a junkie, and it wasn't long before he dropped out of sight. I've tried to find him a couple of times, once by going to the pub in Bolton where drug deals are fairly common, but to no avail. I hope he's okay. Bill Bradbury and some other friends I made at Bolton County Grammar School—Stephen "Hoss" Hey, Pam Hulme, Pete Vickers, Ron Booth, and Lynne Earp—remain friends to this day, and we try to grab a night out in Bolton every now and then. Every four or five years, I guess. I treasure those nights.

Pete Vickers, Bill Bradbury, gaz, and Hoss Hey, 2000.

Back at the Prince Rupert, I got extra spending money for cleaning the beer cellar and the beer pipes every week, and Vi and Bernard also paid me to serve in the small off-license attached to the side of the pub where we sold beer, wine, and spirits to go, as well as candy and used superhero comic books straight from my collection. I'd been reading these things since I was about nine or 10 years old, and although I had more than a couple of favorites, Superman was top of my list. I often think that it was because of Superman that I had a love affair with New York, 'cause we all know that Metropolis was the Big Apple, right?

I stated tending bar at the Prince Rupert when I was about 14 years old, pulling pints for the regulars two or three nights per week, if memory serves, and on Friday and Saturday nights I was allowed to hang out with the staff and a few of the locals when Vi and Bernard hosted a lock-in—a continuation of bar service after the legal closing time has passed. The pub would close at 11 in the P.M., and by midnight there would be anywhere between six and 20 people hanging out at the bar supping more ale. I was allowed shandies—lemon soda and ale—and I had to show Vi how much lemon soda was in my glass before I topped it off with the beer. If it was less that half-full I had to add more soda. I'd yell, "Mum," while holding the glass in the air, and Vi would turn around, nod her approval, then turn back to whoever she was chatting with. I would then drink as much of the soda as I could very quickly and fill the glass with Tetley's bitter. Pub life was most definitely for me.

Serving in the off-license helped me find friends who lived near to the pub—Bolton County Grammar was a twenty-minute bus ride away, and only one lad I knew who lived close to the pub went to the same school as I. It also gave me a feel for the people who lived on the Great Lever Council Estate. Not many of them had much by the way of cash in the bank, but cash in the bank doesn't make a man solid, and for the most part these folk were very solid, indeed.

Although lots of people who lived near the Prince Rupert didn't have much cash to spare, most of them managed to put decent meals on the table three times a day so things weren't real desperate for them. Nevertheless, some of them would tap Bernard on the shoulder for the loan of a five-pound note every now and again, and Bernard would usually come through.

Money wasn't the only thing that the customers at the Prince Rupert used Bernard for, though. He was looked on as a sort of father figure by more than a few of them. Bernard was someone who people would go to whenever they were in a pickle. On more than one occasion the phone rang in the middle of the night and a local said something to the effect of, "Bernard, I think our Billy's dead. I just woke up and I don't think he's breathing. What do I do?" Bernard would call the right people, and he'd go round to the house, too, to sit with the wife while it all went down. He truly cared for the customers at the Prince Rupert, and it showed. The regulars loved him for it.

Vi—and I didn't learn this until just after her death in 2001—slipped cash to one or two people who really needed it, too. The daughter of one of the barmaids, I was told, needed some medical attention not covered by the National Health program, and Vi came up with the cash they needed to sort it out. Bear in mind that we were far from being wealthy, but we probably had a better cash flow than most of the other residents of the council estate.

In return for their generosity and for their genuine concern for their customers, the pub regulars were loyal to Vi and Bernard. Fiercely loyal. No strangers ever started any trouble in the Prince Rupert, and anyone who tried to take advantage of any member of the Regan family was quickly set straight. You wouldn't want to mess with these guys, either. They tended to know how to put a point across. The four years we spent in Bolton turned out to be very important to me in later years. Taught me some core values. That sort of stuff. I'll get to them later, so stick around.

Prince Rupert, circa 1965. Aunt Mary on the left, Nan holding the dog, Dad wearing the fez, Vi's the blonde with the big smile, cousin Ken is at the back to the left of Vi.

For Bernard, the role of the pub landlord came very easily. He was born to play this part. He loved to be the center of attention, and the man had a heart of gold, too. Vi didn't really want to be the landlady of the Prince Rupert. She went back into the pub business because Bernard was miserable, I think, but although I wasn't privy to what went down between them on a personal level when that decision was made, I'd wager heavy that Bernard didn't bully her into it. Vi and Bernard were a true love match.

Vi had been dealing with the public at the dress shop in Cleveleys for over a decade, so she was used to handling people and situations, but pubs are different from dress shops. Although Bernard was completely at home being a pub landlord, Vi wasn't quite sure how to play the role of the landlady. Dad was so much larger-than-life, and Vi had to take a back seat to him yet still command respect from the staff and from the customers. Not an altogether easy task to pull off.

In order to increase business at the pub, Bernard hired a drummer and a piano player. They called themselves Styx and Tones. He hired an emcee who went by the name of Jacko Diamonds, too, and every Wednesday, Friday, and Saturday night this trio put on quite a show. They were all pretty good at what they did. Jacko was a great host—he'd sing a few numbers, then he'd introduce other customers who wanted to perform, and he'd be the one to wrap it up at the end of the night. The last number was always "The Party's Over," a song from *The Bells Are Ringing*, a 1956 musical starring Judy Holliday, and it's been recorded by Nat "King" Cole, Doris Day, Shirley Bassey, and more recently, The Smokin' Popes.

Prince Rupert circa 1966 Styx & Tones with Jacko Diamonds.

The pub was soon packed on Styx and Tones nights, and some of the locals went to great trouble to hone their acts by donning costumes, wearing extravagant stage makeup, and some would bring a guitar or perhaps a harmonica to play. The place ended up with quite a reputation, and Joe "Mr. Piano" Henderson, a national British television personality, came and played the piano for us on one occasion. Various other fairly talented folk performed pop songs, C & W numbers, nostalgic ditties from both the World Wars—"eeh, them were the good old days, weren't they?"—and various Rat-Pack-style songs. "My Way" was a particular favorite. Too bad nobody nailed that one till Sid Vicious came along. The younger end of the crowd sang pop songs—Beatles, Searchers, Cat Stevens, that sort of stuff. No R&B. No Stones or Yardbirds. Pop songs. Stuff that everyone back then, regardless of age, tended to enjoy.

One guy who showed up from time to time went by the name of Blosh. A tough town needs a town tough, someone no one else ever tackles, and nobody in Bolton ever wanted to get on the wrong side of Blosh. Head to toe he measured around five-feet eight. Shoulder to shoulder he was about the same. The man was a cube. His head was shaved bald, and nobody else in a town like Bolton, circa 1966, shaved his head unless he had ringworm.

Blosh would appear at the Prince Rupert about twice a year and the room would go silent when he walked in the door. For a minute or so you might hear his name whispered to the one or two people at the far end of the room who hadn't noticed his entrance. They might be laughing at some stupid joke, but they soon shut up when they saw who had walked into the room. People didn't laugh when Blosh was around. He might think they were laughing at him.

The town tough would stroll up to the bar and order a pint of bitter. Bernard always made sure that he was the one to serve Blosh. He was always very pleasant to this potential troublemaker, not because he was scared of Blosh, but because Bernard knew how to handle the man. He always made sure to look Blosh directly in the eye and to show him some respect. And Blosh would always shake Bernard's hand, smile, and they'd exchange a nicety or two before Blosh took a pull on his pint and strolled across the barroom to have a word in Jacko Diamonds' ear. Two minutes later Jacko would introduce Blosh to the room, and Blosh would make his way onto the stage—a platform just big enough to hold a drum kit, a small upright piano, and one singer—that was raised about eight inches from the floor. In a powerful tenor voice that filled the whole fuckin' room with glory, Blosh would belt out one of the most soul-wrenching renditions of "Danny Boy" you've ever heard. He started out soft. Real soft.

"Oh Danny boy, the pipes, the pipes are calling
From glen to glen, and down the mountain side
The summer's gone, and all the flowers are dying
'tis you, 'tis you must go and I must bide."

He fair bellowed the next verse.

"But come you back when summer's in the meadow
Or when the valley's hushed and white with snow
'tis I'll be there in sunshine or in shadow
Oh Danny boy, oh Danny boy, I love you so."

Back he came for the next verse, way down low again.

"And if you come, when all the flowers are dying
And I am dead, as dead I well may be
You'll come and find the place where I am lying
And kneel and say an 'Ave' there for me."

45

Just a little bit louder now ...

"And I shall hear, tho' soft you tread above me
And all my dreams will warm and sweeter be
If you'll not fail to tell me that you love me
I'll simply sleep in peace until you come to me."

And one last time he repeats that last line. This time he sings it way slow—one word at a time—and at the top of his fuckin' voice. His voice reached the far corners of the fuckin' universe, I swear it.

"I'll
simply
sleep
in
peace
until
you
come
to
me."

Blosh lingered long on that last word. Real long.

When the song was over there wasn't a dry eye in the house. Blosh would finish his pint and he would leave peacefully. He didn't want to fuck up in the only place left in town where he could get some stuff off his chest without actually beating the crap out of someone, so it's probably worth dissecting here what really went down twixt Blosh and Bernard when Blosh graced the Prince Rupert with his presence.

It's probably best that you understand Bernard's intentions, not just when it came to dealing with Blosh, but his intentions in general. My Dad had a built-in sort of mindfulness. He knew how to deal with people, and he was always looking to make people happy. He wasn't a man to be trifled with, mind. Cross him too often, or too badly, and your name would be crossed off his list permanently. But although Bernard was seeking financial success, he did it in the best possible way. Honorably. By attempting to do something that I stress to bartenders today: As far as is possible, try to make sure that everyone who comes into your bar leaves feeling better than they did when they came in. Bernard treated everyone with respect, regardless of what others might have said about certain individuals. And treating Blosh with respect was certainly the way to go.

Anger, I believe—and I'm not alone—is always based in fear, so it's possible that the anger that spewed from Blosh when he picked fights with anyone who looked at him the wrong way was based on his fear of being disrespected. When he saw that Bernard offered him respect, his anger was quelled and he was able to relax a little. I find that now, some forty-odd years later, if I see anger in anyone, it's usually possible to trace that anger back to one fear or another, and when it's seen from that perspective, anger in others can be easier to deal with.

I go into this in more detail in the chapter about Mindful Connections, but this knowledge can serve bartenders well when they have to confront angry customers. Look for the source of their fear, and approach them with that in mind and with love in your heart.

On the nights that Styx and Tones played, if Bernard had enough booze inside of him, and he usually did, he'd wind up on the stage putting all he had into "There's No Business Like Show Business," and if he was in the mood, he'd belt out some old war songs or music-hall ditties, too. One of his very favorites was "The Spaniard That Blighted My Life," a little-known music-hall number that Bernard loved to sing when he'd had a skin-full.

If I catch Alphonso Spagoni, the Toreador,
With one mighty swipe I will dislocate his bally jaw.
I'll fight this bull-fighter I will,
And when I catch the bounder
the blighter I'll kill.
He shall die, he shall die!
He shall die tiddly-i-ti-ti-ti-ti-ti-ti!
He shall die, he shall die!

For I'll raise a bunion on his Spanish onion
If I catch him bending tonight!

Bernard raised hell with this song. The customers whooped and laughed and shouted and screamed and laughed some more. He was a regular superstar on the Great Lever Council Estate, was Bernard. He had a voice, too. Not a voice that could have made a living on its own, but he was easy on the ears all the same. Vi just stood back and watched all this go down. She'd shake her head and smile and say, "Oh, Bernard." Words I heard pretty frequently in the Prince Rupert days, and not just from Vi. Nan was fond of the phrase, too.

While Vi was busy coming to terms with her new position in life, I was learning to bask in the glory of pub life. As the landlord's son I got quite a bit of respect on the street. By the time I was 15 I was staying up till all hours of the morning drinking pints of bitter with the grown-ups and prowling the pubs in the center of town on Fridays with the Five Pints of Bitter Lads, a group of guys around four or five years older than yours truly who hung out at the Rupert and invited me to go out with them on their Friday-night quests to try to get some action from the fairer sex. We walked from pub to pub to pub drinking pints of bitter or Bacardi and Coke when we were a bit flush. Sometimes we ended up at a casino or a nightclub, missing the last bus back to Great Lever and walking home in

the wee hours of Saturday morning. We actually saw Lulu singing "Shout" at the Castle Casino one night.

The Five Pints of Bitter Lads—Dave Ridings, Ian Wilson,
Dirty Bobby, Eddie Kilcoyne, and Johnnie Shields, a good
looking lad who probably could have talked his way into a for-
mal dinner dance wearing a ripped, oil-covered T-shirt—sometimes ended up with women on our nights on the town, but
there weren't any 18-year-old chickies who would look twice at
a 15-year-old boy, even if he did dye his hair grey at the side-
burns so he could get into pubs. God, I was such an asshole.
Not a real obnoxious asshole, but an asshole all the same.

In The Castle Pub, Bolton, circa 1967, with four of the five pints of bitter
lads. Ian Wilson, me, Bobby Wotshisname, and Dave Ridings.

As I remember it, the only time I got close to getting lucky
in this period was with the younger sister of one of the regulars
at the pub whose name escapes me. He and his wife threw a
party, and I ended up staying over and spending the night on
the living room floor with this girl who might have been 17 to

my 15, but I don't really have a clue how old she was, what her name was, or what kind of activities we actually indulged in that night. I remember only that the lads applauded me when I next met up with them for a pint, and that I kept my mouth shut about not remembering what had gone down.

The long arm of the law never did catch me at my underage drinking game, but I had strict instructions on what to do if I was ever collared. In the sixties, the law exonerated whoever served a minor as long as they went to the trouble of asking the customer how old he was. If the kid said he was 18, then it was legal to serve him. Simple as that.

"If the police ever catch you," Vi told me in real serious tones, "You tell them that the landlord asked how old you were. You don't go getting other people into trouble. Okay?" Vi didn't lay the law down too often and I had a pretty freewheeling youth, so when she threw stuff like this at me I knew I'd better listen. She'd never ever have laid a hand on me, but disappointing Vi would have been way more painful than a beating.

My grades at school, as you might imagine, were not too good, but I didn't really care too much, either. I was passing most of my exams but only by the skin of my teeth, and I got some wonderful comments from my teachers on my report cards. "Cheerful, helpful, and noisy," was, perhaps, my favorite. It came from Doctor Roberts, the headmaster.

I was pretty popular at Bolton County Grammar School, and I played drums in a band called The Sons of Adam, along with Stephen "Hoss" Hey (bass), Johnny Nichols (the tough kid who was also a Mick Jagger-wannabe), Pete Vickers (keyboard), and Roger "Tosh" Ball (lead guitar). I was probably the worst musician of this motley crew, but I had a drum set and Vi and Bernard allowed us to practice in the pub on Saturday afternoons, so I was a shoe-in for the job. We played one gig, at a high-school dance. We were the opening act for The Rebels, a pretty good band in which our classmate, Chris Whitham, played guitar. The Sons of Adam were not well received.

I had a few girlfriends during this period. Linda Barlow, a girl in my class, was the first, and she was followed by Judy Roper, who was one year older than I. I had a fling with Pam Hulme on a school vacation to Italy, and although she dumped me when we got home, the fling was pretty fabulous while it lasted. Eventually, the beer started to give me a belly, and although I wasn't turning into a real fat kid, I was overweight, and that didn't help when I was looking for a date.

When I was 16 going on 17, Vi and Bernard snagged The Bay Horse. It was the pub of Bernard's dreams. The Bay was a true Olde Worlde pub in a 400-plus-year-old building, complete with authentic beams, horse brasses, and pewter tankards that belonged to eight or 10 of the regulars hanging behind the main bar. It suited Dad down to the ground. The pub stands on the main road in Thornton, close to a bunch of shops, about four miles from the sea-front. I picked up old friendships when we moved back to the coast, but I still managed to stay in touch with some of my pals from Bolton. We didn't leave the Great Lever Council Estate without Bernard throwing one last big-time bash for the regulars at the Prince Rupert, though.

Nigh-on everyone who'd ever set foot in the pub over those four years was there on Vi and Bernard's last night. Pint after pint after pint crossed the bar, and it took half a dozen of us to keep the glasses full. We tried not to break anything. Bernard had posted a notice over the sink: "Due to the rising prices of bandages, would members of staff please try not to cut themselves while breaking glasses."

Closing time came at 11 in the P.M. Bernard locked the front door and the party carried on. And on. And on. At about two o'clock in the morning the police arrived. The police liked Bernard and Vi since they got free beer at the Prince Rupert if they tapped on the window after hours, but on this occasion it was official business. "You've got to keep the noise down, Bernard. We're getting complaints," the officers told Dad. Bernard got everyone to keep their voices down, pulled a couple of pints for the cops, and the party carried on. Two hours later Bernard had to call the police station. "I think you'd better send another car to the Prince Rupert," he told the officer on duty. The cops were way too drunk to drive.

I learned much about the booze business during our four years at the Prince Rupert. Indeed, Bernard always told me that the pub would serve as the completion of my education, so when I dropped out of high school that same year we moved back to the seaside, I believed I was fully equipped to take on the world at large.

Attaining passing grades in five subjects, including math and English, used to be the equivalent of graduating high school in the USA. With five O-levels you could get a job in a bank. Stay at high school for another two years and get yourself three or more A-levels, and you stood a chance of going on to university. My three O-levels, in geography, math, and domestic science (cooking), might have gotten me an interview for a job at a chip shop, but I didn't care. I was a very happy drinking man who knew that one day I'd own a chain of restaurants. My Dad had made out well with little education. So would I.

So what did I really learn while hanging out and tending bar at the Prince Rupert? When you work behind a bar, whether as a pub landlord or landlady or as a bartender, the most important aspect of your job is caring about your customers. And you must care in a very real sense, and on a very personal level.

The fact is, you see, that nobody ever goes to a pub or a bar for a drink. Why would they? They can drink at home, right? People go to bars for all sorts of reasons. They go to get laid, they go to meet a business partner, they go for conversation, they go to celebrate, they go to cry on someone's shoulder, but they never, never, ever go to a bar for a drink.

This is the message—the lesson—that I'm still spouting to young bartenders in the twenty-first century. It's not something I take lightly. In the section on Mindful Bartending, coming up next, you'll see where this philosophy, drummed into me at a very early age, has taken me.

I CAN AND DO MAKE GOOD PUNCH, BECAUSE I DO NOTHING ELSE

"The man who sees, does, or thinks of anything else while he is making Punch may as well look for the Northwest Passage on Mutton Hill. A man can never make good punch unless he is satisfied, nay positive, that no man breathing can make better. I can and do make good Punch, because I do nothing else, and this is my way of doing it. I retire to a solitary corner with my ingredients ready sorted; they are as follows, and I mix them in the order they are here written. Sugar, twelve tolerable lumps; hot water, one pint; lemons, two, the juice and peel; old Jamaica rum, two gills; brandy, one gill; porter or stout, half a gill; arrack, a slight dash. I allow myself five minutes to make a bowl in the foregoing proportions, carefully stirring the mixture as I furnish the ingredients until it actually foams; and then Kangaroos! how beautiful it is!"

Popular Fallacies by Charles Lamb, 1826.

The Mindful Bartender

> "Almost anyone can learn to mix drinks accurately and fast. That is the least of it. I have always believed success behind the bar comes from an ability to understand the man or woman I am serving, to enter into his joys or woes, make him feel the need of me as a person rather than a servant."
>
> This Must be the Place: Memoirs of Jimmie the Barman, by Morrill Cody, 1937.

You might have heard the term *mindfulness* quite often in the recent past. It's associated with Buddhism, though you certainly don't need to be a Buddhist to practice mindfulness. Atheists, Agnostics, Christians, Hindus, Jews, Moslems, and anyone else on the face of the earth can practice mindfulness. And lots of bartenders have been practicing mindfulness for years, though they might not be familiar with the term.

Personally, I've been learning about mindfulness primarily from a woman named **Sandy Wells**. Sandy conducts a Sunday-morning meditation in my home town in the Hudson Valley, and recently she's been focusing on mindfulness. After learning about this concept it quickly became clear to me that the craft of the bartender lends itself beautifully to mindfulness, so I decided to try to adapt the philosophy to our craft, and Sandy, along with **Martha Schueneman**, my mindful editor, helped guide me. Thanks guys.

I've also been working with **Aisha Sharpe** of New York's **Contemporary Cocktails** company, and **Dushan Zaric**, from **Employees Only** and **The Macao Trading Company**, two fabulous bars in the Big Apple, to put together a program on this subject. Aisha and Dushan have been conducting bartender workshops on *The Mastery of Wisdom*, a related subject, for quite some time, and together we have formed *The Institute for Mindful Bartending*, a concept that's in its infancy, and will always be, I think, a work in progress.

I don't purport to be a qualified teacher of mindfulness. I merely want to pass along what I've been learning for the past few years, and make some suggestions on how you might want to put mindfulness to work for you both behind the bar and as part of your daily life. Mindfulness has brought much happiness into my life, and I'm hoping to spread the joy a little. In my opinion, mindfulness isn't something to achieve, it's something to keep working on. I doubt if many, or any, people are fully mindful 24/7, but people who embrace mindfulness, from my point of view, seem to be very happy people. I believe that a brand new Lamborghini might make you happy for a few hours, but mindfulness can make you happy for the rest of your life.

Before we get down to the nitty gritty, then, let me add one more thing. Mindfulness, in my opinion, is like a tailored suit. The suit has to have lapels, but you get to decide how wide they are. Trousers are mandatory, but cuffs are your call. Similarly, everyone gets to pick and choose what suits them best on the path of mindfulness. Take a look, consider your options, and take whatever you're comfortable with. A little mindfulness is better than none at all, I think. And above all, though, no matter what anyone tells you, don't ever take things too seriously. We're here to have fun, you know. You can't be happy and too serious at the same time!

Becoming a Mindful Bartender

Mindfulness, when applied to tending bar, is an approach to the job that entails being totally aware of everything you are doing, being cognizant of everything that is going on around you, and tuning in to all of your guests' wants and needs. You can also be mindful of your mixology skills, and we'll discuss this a little later in this chapter. Be aware that mindfulness is not easy. It's something that, should you decide to try become a mindful bartender, you will never 100-percent achieve in this lifetime. It's worth striving for, though.

A mindful bartender trusts her intuition. She is primarily focused on what the customer in front of her is doing or saying, or upon the drink she is making, but she is also aware of what's going on at the other end of the bar, and in the entire restaurant. She keeps tabs on the atmosphere of the place, and she constantly monitors the events, actions, and people that might affect the mood at the bar or within the restaurant. A mindful bartender pays attention to the personal preferences of her guests, and she makes each person's drinks accordingly. A mindful bartender leaves her personal shit at the door because she knows she can't be fully attentive to her customers if she's obsessing about the fight she just had with her sister or if she's making mental notes about all the crap she needs to do tomorrow morning before her spin class. A mindful bartender sets her intentions to be of service to her customers.

Mindful bartenders draw customers to their bars like bears to a honey-pot, and their customers always feel better for having visited them. Since more customers results in more money in the tip-cup, mindful bartenders are rewarded monetarily for their efforts, and since more customers also results in more money in the cash register, bar owners take extra special care of their mindful bartenders.

This all leads to a great atmosphere in bars where mindful bartenders work, and mindful bartenders spend far less time pounding the pavement because they quit that lousy job or that bastard fired them for no good reason. Mindful bartenders are highly valued workers in the hospitality industry.

There are a number of different ways to approach mindfulness behind the bar, and I'll attempt to explain these in relatively simple terms in this section. I'm keeping it simple because I'm not sure that I understand mindfulness in its entirety, though there are times when it all falls into place for me. I read a book once that explained Einstein's Theory of Relativity in such simple terms that, for about three minutes, I swear I understood it. Then it was gone. For me, mindfulness is like that, too.

First, though, we have to understand something about intuition, and acceptance of certain universal truths that aren't quite tangible.

Do you remember the last time that your gut told you not to serve someone but you went ahead and did anyway? You regretted that one, right? Have you ever walked into a room where a couple has been arguing, and although they "snap out of it" and make like nothing was going down, you could feel the tension in the atmosphere? Have you ever gotten the feeling that someone is looking at you, and when you turned your head, sure enough, you see someone with their eyes glued to you?

If you answered *yes* to any of those questions, and I'm betting that most people answer all in the affirmative, then I'm going to ask you to bear that sense of intuition in mind as you read this section. We might not be able to take a picture of our intuition, but it's there. The universe send us signs constantly, and those signs, if we take notice of them and if we act on them, can help us lead happier, healthier lives. Taking notice of how we feel about serving a drink to someone who might have already had enough, and acting on that feeling by refusing service, for instance, will ultimately lead to you feeling happier than you would have felt had you served him. There might be a bit of a scene if the prospective customer becomes belligerent, but it won't be anywhere near as bad as things could get if you hand him another drink. One more drink and this guy might start annoying your other customers, he could start a fight, or, well, you know how that goes.

If you don't already do this, think about casting your eyes over everyone at the bar on a regular basis, and if you can see the tables in the restaurant, try to find time to look at the people there, too. Naturally this will help you become aware of who needs your attention, but it will also pay off by giving you some guidance as to what's going down at the bar, and in the restaurant. It's fairly easy to understand the body language that people display, so by doing this, and by trusting the vibes you get as you look around, all sorts of problems can be avoided. The vibes might not be as strong as they are when you walk into a room right after a heated argument, but they are there all the same, and it's not too hard to tap into them.

And you can also use your intuition, and/or your powers of observation, to start trying to understand why each of your guests have come to your bar. Sometimes this can be very ob-vious. A guy who asks to send a drink to the single woman down the bar is obviously out to meet someone, right? And two women talking about hiring a new office manager are at the bar to talk business, while the man buying the bar a drink to toast the birth of his new baby is obviously there to celebrate. Now think about how you're going to treat these people. You might ask the woman if she would like to accept a drink from the guy looking to meet someone new, and you should be ready to let him down lightly if she refuses. You'll probably be protective of the two businesswomen by not trying to make small-talk with them, and being on the look-out for anyone who approaches them with that sort of thing in mind. And the man with a new baby will love you for letting him buy the bar a drink, then giv-ing him a nice cognac on the house along with a big smile and a hearty congratulations.

Trusting your intuition, or your gut-reaction, then, is a very important aspect of mindfulness. And learning to act on how certain people or situations make you feel is something to strive for. These things come naturally to many bartenders, but not to *all* bartenders. Those of you who find this sort of thing difficult, though, needn't fret. Relax, make an effort, and your efforts will be rewarded. Promise.

NOT HALF SO INNOCENT
AS IT TASTES

"Kentucky whiskey, says John Burroughs, is soft, seductively so, and I caution all travellers to beware how they suck any iced preparation of it through a straw, of a hot day; it is not half so innocent as it tastes."

The Legends of the St. Lawrence: Told During a Cruise of the Yatch Hirondelle from Montreal to Gaspe by James MacPherson Le Moine, F.R.S.C., 1898.

Mindful Connections

Connecting mindfully to customers at your bar can be rewarding in many different ways, but to be a mindful bartender you must also connect to yourself, becoming aware of your thoughts, being careful not to judge others, and being particularly careful about which words you choose to use when you connect verbally with others. And if you want to reap the full benefits of mindfulness, treat the dishwasher the same way you treat your guests at the bar, and treat that homeless guy you've been avoiding the same way, too. Living a mindful life, as you will see if you pursue it, is a very rewarding venture.

Preparation for Mindfulness: Ten Minutes of Hush and Wonder

> [The cocktail hour] is the violet hour, the hour of hush and wonder, when the affectations glow and valor is reborn, when the shadows deepen along the edge of the forest and we believe that, if we watch carefully, at any moment we may see the unicorn." –The Hour by Bernard DeVoto, 1948.

In 1973, when I first started tending bar in New York, I was more than a little intimidated by my customers. I was a small-town guy from a seaside resort in the northwest of England, and New Yorkers seemed to be larger than life to me. New Yorkers had so much confidence in themselves. They were far faster on their feet than the customers at pubs in the U.K. that I'd left in order to start a new life in the Big Apple. And of course, once they sussed out that I was little cowed by them, they took advantage of that at every opportunity.

Every night, then, when I got to work at Drake's Drum, the joint on the Upper East Side that gave me my first break in the Big Apple, I was nervous about interacting with these people and having to be in control of the bar. With this in mind, I arrived at the Drum at least an hour before my shift began. I took a table on my own, ordered dinner, and I refused to let anyone join me. As I quietly ate my dinner, I composed myself so that, when I got behind the bar, I would be ready to face the crowd. When I finished eating I would continue to sit alone, absorbing the mood of the bar and telling myself that I was going to have a great night.

I was, in effect, meditating and setting my intention, though I didn't know that at the time. And my nightly practice of achieving solitude in a crowded room paid off well. I was no longer intimidated by the customers, and as a result of that, the customers were more respectful of me. This had a snowball effect, and I was soon loving being the center of attraction behind the bar, and although the customers still teased me—and that's true to this day; it's the way in which I like to be treated—they did it with love, and I played along with it, zinging them back whenever it seemed appropriate.

Why I started my ritual of an hour of quietness, or stillness, before my shift began I have no idea. I knew nothing of meditation, or mindfulness, or Buddhism, or anything else related to this practice at the time. I remember doing it, though, and I remember it working for me very well indeed. Some sort of meditation, I believe, is crucial to being a mindful bartender. It helps you to focus on what you are about to do, it gives you time to set your intentions to be of service to others, and it helps to center you so you can be aware of everything that's going on around you.

In order to be mindful, then, think about taking a little time—five to 10 minutes should do it—to sit quietly on your own and set your intentions for the night ahead. If you can't do this at work, then do it before you leave your home. If you don't want anyone at home to see you meditating, the bathroom's always a safe place for solitude.

There's no need to sit in a lotus position in order to meditate, though it's easier if you are in a seated position and if you are totally comfortable. Now sit quietly on your own, and try to become aware of yourself. Close your eyes and pay attention to your breath. Feel the cool air coming into your nostrils, and be aware of the warm breath as it leaves your mouth or your nose. Try thinking, "I'm breathing in. I'm breathing out." When your mind drifts, and you start thinking, "Oh shit, it's Thursday night and that means that that asshole Sam will be here later on," try to avoid holding onto the thought and following it. Just watch that thought float by and go back to, "I'm breathing in. I'm breathing out."

Some people use their own mantras when mediating, so you might want to come up with some words of your own in order to center yourself, or you could use the so-hum mantra, thinking *so* as you breath in, and *hum* as you exhale. I learned that one from Deepak Chopra who says that it's been used for thousands of years by Indians, Native Americans, and Australian Aborigines.

You can set a timer for five, 10, or 15 minutes to bring you out of your meditation, or you can simply return to the physical world when you feel the time is right. The universe will guide you on this. And as you open your eyes and come back to what we think of as *reality*, it's good to set your intentions for your shift. There's nothing wrong with intending to make lots of money, but that will come to you automatically if you set your intentions to be of service to others, to make your guests happy, to brighten the day or the evening of those around you, and to bring a little sunshine into everyone whose life you touch when you're behind the bar.

Meditation, or stillness, isn't the only way of preparing for a shift, and if you just can't get your head around the concept, other forms of preparation might work for you. Loud music works for me, for instance, and when I've been alone in a bar, setting up for the first shift of the day, I've often found that playing the right playlist—which can be anything from Krisna Das to Gogol Bordello—at the right volume can help center me and get me ready for my shift. For me, loud music *can be* a form of meditation, and I know I'm not alone in this. The music blocks out that constant conversation in my mind, and I'm able to focus, and set my intentions.

If you do this, you'll quickly notice that you're better able to cope with whatever comes your way during your hours behind the bar. You'll deal with potentially troublesome customers with more understanding, you'll treat your co-workers with a better sense of camaraderie, and you might even end up understanding why your boss can be so negative at times. She's just not very mindful, right?

The practice of meditation, then, no matter how you do it, and the setting of good, honorable intentions, will serve you well. And you'll see a difference in your work-life in a very short time, indeed.

Mindful Communication

Communication is integral to the bartender's job. It's of the utmost importance that we make a real connection when we interact with others. Try to remember that communication is a two-way street, and listening is every bit as important as talking. Mindful people listen intently to what's being said to them, and they make sure that the person who is talking to them is aware that they are being heard loud and clear.

When you enter into a conversation with a guest, say, even if the purpose of the tête-à-tête is just to take an order for drinks, the mindful bartender will always look into the eyes of her guests as they are speaking to her. Even if the guest is looking elsewhere, mindful bartenders pay attention to the eyes of whoever is talking to them. More often than not, this will cause the customer to turn his head to look at the bartender. He will *feel* her gaze, and when he realizes that the bartender is focusing all of her attention on him, the relationship between the two parties will change for the better.

Mindful bartenders think, too, about how they communicate with their co-workers. Not just the other bartenders, but also the boss, the waitstaff, the chef, and the dishwasher. When they greet any of their co-workers, providing there's time to do this, mindful bartenders look into their eyes, ask them how they are doing, and they *wait for a reply.* Listening to people's answers is a very important part of mindfulness. It's also good to understand that in many cases, dishwashers, kitchen porters, and people whose hourly rate is minimal at best, are pretty much invisible while they are at work. They are taken for granted, and few people give them the time of day. Mindful bartenders who make an effort to communicate mindfully with these people are usually rewarded immediately with a look that tells them *thanks for taking 30 seconds to talk to me, everyone else ignores me.*

Bartenders who communicate mindfully with their co-workers end up working in fabulous environments. The mindfulness becomes infectious, and it soon travels throughout the staff, resulting in a true team of people who care about each other's well-being. And there are practical advantages to this sort of behavior, too. If a mindful bartender is truly in the weeds, she can count on almost anyone on the staff to help her out. The waiter will bring ice, the dishwasher will run to the store for lemons, and the line cook will cut twists for her whenever she's slammed behind the bar.

You might want to think about using mindful communication outside of the workplace, too. Next time you ask, say, the check-out person or grocery bagger at the supermarket how they're doing, try looking them dead in the eye, and stay that way until they finish their reply, then react. I recently asked a tech-support guy (on the phone) how he was doing, and he told me about how down he was because his favorite basketball player just got traded to a team he didn't like. I listened, commiserated, and told him that, although I don't follow basketball, I know how upset I get when my favorite bartenders go to work at bars that I can't easily get to. We both had a chuckle, and he proceeded to handle my problem with a great attitude and the utmost efficiency. Okay, he might have done that anyway, but for the sake of no more than 60 seconds, we two human beings connected, shared a laugh, and our days got just a little bit brighter. When people know that you're interested in whatever it is they have to say, they will always react in a very favorable manner. I've heard it said that Bill Clinton got laid a lot at college because he listened intently to whatever his dates had to say, so it's got to be worth a try, right?

And if you really want to take this to the streets, you might want to think about trying this with homeless people who are holding out their cups for your spare change. As you give them as much as you can afford, look them in the eye, ask them how they are doing, and listen to their answers. You'll be amazed at the very interesting conversations you'll end up having with some, though not all, of these people. Sometimes homeless folk give you a glimpse into a world that you'd prefer not to know about. One homeless guy said to me, "You're the first person today not to treat me like an asshole." Can you imagine going through that day after day? Can you imagine how good he made me feel by telling me that? This sort of thing can be very rewarding, indeed, for both parties.

Martha, my editor, gave me a hard time about the previous paragraph, saying, "this comes across here as vaguely blowing-your-own-horn, like, you're doing this so that people will make *you* feel good." And she's right. To a point. I wasn't attempting to blow my own horn, I was illustrating how *everyone* benefits from mindfulness. I don't believe that there's anything wrong with reaping the rewards of mindfulness. In my opinion, we're here on earth to be happy, so I grab happiness wherever I find it. I felt good when the guy told me that I'd brightened his day a little, and his words had also given me a glimpse into a world that I don't understand, so we both emerged richer for this very short encounter with each other. What's wrong with that? I also give money to charity, not *only* so the charity will help people needier than I, but also because I know that the universe will reward me with more money. I've been doing this only for the past four or five years, and it has worked well for me thus far.

Whatever you take away from this chapter, please think about practicing mindful behavior when you're dealing with just about everyone you meet. The woman at the gas station, the guy from whom you buy the newspaper in the morning, and the barista who makes your morning cup of joe down at the corner coffee joint. Start out by watching how he gets treated by the people ahead of you in the queue—most of them will barely acknowledge his existence. Then, when it's your turn, look him in the eye, smile large, ask him, "How's *your* day going so far?" And once again, keep looking at him so that he knows that you're waiting to hear his answer.

When you practice mindful communication during every encounter you have with another human being, life on this planet gets to be so much sweeter. And it happen, more or less, instantaneously. Promise.

Mindful Phrasing

No matter how you feel about this, you should always do what I'm about to tell you to do.

How did that last sentence make you feel? Not too good, huh? Of course it didn't feel good. I have no right whatsoever to tell you what you should and should not do. You are the only person who can decide that sort of thing. You might want to think about this though... .

Telling people that they might want to *think about* doing this or that is a delightful way of pointing out their options without dictating what they *should* or *should not* do.

"I wonder if you could think about lowering your voice just a little, please," for instance, usually works far better than, "Hey, you, keep your voice down." Rather than telling guests what to do, offer them a chance to make up their own mind.

We've seen how important listening is to mindful communication. Mindful phrasing is how you speak with others. When you choose your words carefully—both what you say and how you say it—to reflect the intention you have set, you'll find that people may be more receptive to what you have to say.

Try to remember at all times that words are very powerful. Sticks and stones might break your bones, but words can be far more dangerous. Before you open your mouth, then, it's good to think about what you're going to say, and check that you are going to phrase the sentence mindfully. If you happen to be confronting an angry person, for instance, he or she will, in all probability, misconstrue your intentions if you're not careful about what you say, and a situation that could have been easily remedied can grow out of control very fast.

One phrase that I found worked very well, indeed, when I was handling potentially ugly situations, was, "I need your help." It works like a charm. Say that a guy is coming on to a woman at the bar and she gives you a look that says *help!* You know that you have to do something, but how do you start the ball rolling? Try this: "Excuse me sir, but I'm wondering if you could, perhaps, help me with something? If you'll just come down to the end of the bar I'll explain." Get him on his own so he doesn't lose face, then make up something. "If her boyfriend comes in and sees you, she'll get into big trouble, and she's just too sweet to tell you," or some such thing.

Or maybe you've got a group of half-a-dozen friends who are getting way too loud. Try picking the person who you perceive to be the ringleader and use the very same line on her. Tell her that you need her help, then get her on her own so that she doesn't lose face, then you could think about asking her if she could get her friends to either keep it down or perhaps they could move on to another joint. If you make it plain that it's them, not her, who are the problem, then the situation might resolve itself very quickly.

Don't take my suggestions for what to say too literally—every situation is different, and it's up to you to find the exact right words to use when you're interacting with guests. Trust your intuition, act from a position of love, and you'll be guided to say the right thing.

Anger, Assholes, and Attitude: A Mindful Approach

You can't afford to get angry when you're behind the bar, but no matter how well you understand that, anger will arise on occasion, so let's take a look at how to deal with it. The best lesson I ever saw on this subject came from Sandy Wells, founder of The Institute for Mindful Living, and a woman who has been my personal teacher and guide for the past five years or more. Here is Sandy's take on what you might want to think about doing when you feel yourself getting angry:

Stop

Take a Breath

Open and Observe (Investigate)

Practice Mindful Awareness until you can Proceed without Reactivity

The first two steps are pretty self explanatory, right? When you feel yourself getting angry, stop and become aware of it, and then, rather than exploding, figuratively "count to ten," instead. Try to remember your intentions. Think back to the short meditation you did before your shift began and see if you can recapture that tranquility.

To "Open and Observe" refers to trying to get a grasp on exactly why you are angry. Investigate the cause of it so you can choose the right words for the situation at hand. In order to get your mind around "Practicing Mindful Awareness until you can Proceed without Reactivity," it's important to learn a little more about anger, and where it comes from.

73

In almost all circumstances, anger is based in fear. When you get angry with your boss, it's possibly because you fear that you're powerless in a particular situation. And that might be true, but it's nothing to be afraid of. She has the upper hand *in this particular situation*, and you'll find that if you let her win— it *is* her joint, after all—then the situation will likely right itself very nicely indeed. If your anger comes from getting stiffed by a customer, then is it possible that your anger rises from a fear of being disrespected rather than a fear of becoming penniless? After all, you know darned well that, by the end of your work week, your tips will have evened themselves out. Ain't that always the case? The really good news on the anger issue is this: If you can pull yourself back from the anger, guess what? You won't be angry. And not being angry feels real good.

Someone recently took advantage of me financially, for example, and just as I was about to explode I thought to myself, "It's only money. Let it go." Then I smiled. It felt so much better to let it go than to be angry. And before you jump to any conclusions, you should know that this was a chunk of money that I could not afford to lose at the time. Guess what, though? I got a gig the following week and made more than three times the amount than I usually charged for the type of work I'd be doing. I raised my rates immediately, and I've been getting that kind of money ever since. The universe takes care of what needs to be taken care of.

And by the way, when I didn't get angry at the person who cheated me out of that money, she had no idea how to react towards me—and I must admit that that was a little bit rewarding, too! When people do things to upset us, it throws them off balance a little when we don't get upset back at them. Next time that pompous asshole treats you like his personal manservant, then, play Jeeves to his Wooster and see how he reacts. I'll bet you he starts to lighten up pretty quickly. And never forget that being angry with someone doesn't hurt them in the slightest. It just hurts you. Am I right, or am I right?

If you manage not to get angry when you're a work, that's fabulous. But you will most certainly come up against angry customers, and you've got to know how to deal with anger when it's someone else's. Remember what we just learned: Anger is almost always a result of fear.

When one guy accidentally spills a drink onto another guy, the spillee, as it were, will often get very angry. This sort of thing can lead to physical fights, but if you understand that the spillee's anger is a result of his fear that he'll look like an asshole if he doesn't stand up for himself, then you'll find the situation easier to handle. "Excuse me guys, but this sort of thing happens almost every night in here—it's a bar, and shit happens. Think we could put it all behind us if I buy both of you a drink and pay for your dry cleaning?" is the sort of phrasing that works like a charm. And I heard of one guy who did something similar while pointing a banana at two guys who were about to erupt: "Don't make me use this," he said. Humor works like a charm, too, and who could stop themselves from laughing at such a silly scenario?

Whenever you witness anger, then, the first question to ask yourself is, *what is this person afraid of?* Once you identify that, you're way ahead of the game when it comes to quelling the situation.

My Editor Says That the Following Paragraph Is Important So I'm Adding This Header to Draw Your Attention to It.

Finally, it's good to know that there's a secret to never getting angry, and in order to tap into it all you need to understand is this: Just as anger is always a result of fear, so is happiness always based in love. If you approach life with love in your heart, if you go to any and every situation that goes down in your bar with the intention of seeing past what might appear to be nasty, and seeing instead that love can prevail, then you'll always end up guiding the situation to the happiest ending possible. Love and Fear are the bases for all our other emotions. Fear results in anger; Love brings happiness.

Mindful Mixology

"Mixed drinks might be compared to music; an orchestra will produce good music, provided all players are artists; but have only one or two inferior musicians in your band, and you may be convinced they will spoil the entire harmony."–The Flowing Bowl by William "The Only William" Schmidt, 1892.

If mindful communication stems from an awareness of the other person, which may well be based on your intuition or a hunch, mindful mixology is based in an awareness of flavors and an intuition about which ones might blend harmoniously. Mindful bartenders combine this knowledge of flavors and trust their intuition to create balanced cocktails that suit their customers' palates and preferences.

It's unrealistic to think that any of us will ever know the flavor profiles of every ingredient under the sun, though the consummate professional will try to keep as up to date as possible in this respect. That said, let's spend a couple of minutes to think about what the phrase *achieving balance* means.

The flavors of every ingredient in any given drink will be discernible in a well-balanced cocktail, but let's not take the word *discernible* too literally here. I'd challenge anyone to list the ingredients in, say, a Mai Tai if the drink was presented to them in a blind tasting, but the Mai Tai is a good drink to look at when we discuss balance. After all, it might be hard to pinpoint the curaçao in a Mai Tai, but if you make the drink without the curaçao, you'll immediately know exactly what that ingredient brings to the party.

A well-balanced drink might come to you in the form of a recipe written by a good mixologist, who has detailed specific amounts and bottlings of each and every ingredient. But how do you go about achieving balance if you're presented with a more generic formula, calling merely for, say, tequila, ginger liqueur, and lemon juice, or if you're trying to create a new drink and you have some ingredients in mind but you're not sure what ratios to use?

Mindful mixology involves trusting your intuition whether you're making drinks or creating new recipes, and you're going to be amazed at how easy this is. You're going to have to believe in yourself through and through if you want this to work. I taught this method of mindful mixology for seven years when I held my Cocktails in the Country bartender workshops, and I rarely saw it fail. Here's how it works:

Take the ingredients for a drink that you're fairly familiar with, but use bottlings that you don't know very well. This way you are looking to put ingredients together in harmony, and while you have an understanding of the drink in question, you'll be working with ingredients that you don't know intimately.

Pour 15 ml (.5 ounce) of each ingredient into a shot glass or a sherry copita glass if you prefer.

Have your shaker and ice close at hand.

Taste each ingredient, then immediately make the drink, trusting that your intuition will guide your hands and that you'll achieve balance on the very first try.

That's it. It's as simple as that. Now try using the same procedure using ingredients that you're thinking of using to create a new drink. This won't work every time because your formula hasn't yet been tested, but you'll quickly understand which ingredients are working in the drink, and which ones were a mistake. It's a sure-fire—well, let's say it has over a 90-percent success rate—way of mixing drinks by trusting yourself, your palate, and your mixology skills.

Recipes and Ratios: Nothing Is Written in Stone

"Being bartender and a musician, I compare a classic song to the classic cocktail. For example, we have all heard Wilson Pickett's original classic version of "Mustang Sally." We also have heard cover bands play this song. The cover band offers a rendition of this song–their own interpretation, so to speak. As a musician, I will master the original song, note for note. I may stick with the original arrangement or I may choose to offer my own twist, still following the original score, but adding something of my own. Same thing goes for when I am mixing. If the audience–my bar guest–wants to taste the original, I will fulfill their request with a smile. If they want an added chorus or verse, then I present my interpretation of the classic."–**Angie Jackson**, Ultimate Elixirs, Chicago, 2010.

Unless a cocktail recipe details exact bottlings of every ingredient within the drink, it's best to look at recipes as merely guidelines. Not everyone will agree with me on this point, so I'll ask you to consider my reasons for believing this to be true.

There are people who say that the amount of each ingredient in original recipes should be honored at all times, and in the case of recipes that detail specific bottlings of each ingredient, I agree. To a point. There's nothing wrong with altering ratios a little to suit a specific customer's taste. And to those who say, for instance, that an Aviation must be made to the exact recipe found in Hugo R. Ensslin's 1917 book, *Recipes for Mixed Drinks* (first known printed reference), I say, "that's pure bull." For starters, Ensslin specified using Old Bart gin, which is now defunct, but even if it was still around, the chances of it tasting the same way it tasted in 1917 are remote. Recipes are guidelines. It's a pure and simple fact (in the vast majority of cases). I'll leave you with this thought on the subject: When you make a Béarnaise sauce, do you go looking for Chef Jules Colette's nineteenth-century recipe? Of course not.

Now let's look at some specifics. If a recipe for a Manhattan calls for 60 ml (2 oz) of straight rye and 30 ml (1 oz) of sweet vermouth, imagine how the drink will change with different ryes. Use Rittenhouse Rye @ 50% abv in one drink, then pour a second Manhattan using the Thomas H. Handy Sazerac bottling, which comes in at cask strength, usually well over 65% abv.

Now make another two Manhattans, this time using, say, Michter's 10-year-old rye in both, but make one drink with Martini & Rossi sweet vermouth and use Carpano Antica Formula in the other. They taste completely different from one another, right? The Rittenhouse Manhattan worked well, but the Handy Manhattan was way too strong. You need less whiskey and more vermouth when you're using a 65% abv whiskey. And in the case of the two Michter's Manhattans, the one that called for Martini & Rossi vermouth works well, but the Carpano Antica Formula takes over the glass in the second Manhattan. When you use that particular vermouth you need more whiskey and less vermouth.

The question that we now run up against is this: How do I figure out the correct ratios for making this drink with any given bottling? The object, after all, is to achieve balance in each and every drink, and that's nigh-on impossible if you don't have an intimate knowledge of the flavor profile of every ingredient you're about to work with. Your mission, then, is to keep tasting new ingredients, keep going back to re-taste ingredients you tasted previously, and to constantly learn and re-learn flavor profiles of the bottling you work with. It's an ongoing, life-long process.

Mindful Fulfillment

"An efficient bartender's first aim should be to please his customers, paying particular attention to meet the individual wishes of those whose tastes and desires he has already watched and ascertained; and, with those whose peculiarities he has had no opportunity of learning, he should politely inquire how they wish their beverages served, and use his best judgment in endeavoring to fulfill their desires to their entire satisfaction. In this way he will not fail to acquire popularity and success." The Bar-Tender's Guide or How to Mix all Kinds of Plain and Fancy Drinks by Jerry Thomas, 1887.

Not long ago I went to a new-ish cocktail bar that sported a fabulous menu, and I sat across from a very well-respected bartender whom I've known for a few years. I didn't order my usual Manhattan with lotsa bitters, but instead I chose another strong whiskey-based drink that I'd never before tried. It was fabulous. The bartender then asked if he could make me a drink that he'd created that he thought I'd enjoy, and of course I said yes. That drink was fabulous, too, but it wasn't the sort of thing I'd ever in my life order. Too much citrus for me, and not enough spirit. The bartender wasn't being mindful of my tastes.

In the late 1990s, **Martha Schueneman**, the aforementioned editor of this book who also tended bar for a few years and worked with me on the Cocktails in the Country series, told me about a couple who had walked into her bar and ordered Manhattans. "How do you like your Manhattans?" she enquired, and they proceeded to tell her what whiskey they preferred, what ratio of whiskey to vermouth they used when they made the drink at home, and they added that they didn't use bitters but instead they liked a spoonful of juice from the maraschino cherry jar in their Manhattans. Martha made the drinks exactly the way they instructed, and the couple declared them to be the best they had ever tasted outside of their house. Martha had won two new customers, and you can bet that they told their friends about their favorite bartender.

"Suppose they come back and want something different?" I posed to Martha. "What are you going to make for them?"

"I dunno," she said.

"They like maraschino cherry juice," I said. "And maraschino cherry juice tastes like almonds. Amaretto tastes like almonds, too. Make them something with whiskey and amaretto. A Stiletto, perhaps, if they don't mind the lime juice, or you could go for a simple Godfather made with their favorite whiskey instead of scotch." That's Mindful Fulfillment: Paying attention to the customers preferences so you can fulfill their needs and desires.

You might also want to try up-selling when you practice Mindful Fulfillment. If you know that someone likes Johnnie Walker Gold Label scotch, for instance, you might think about turning them onto Clynelish single malt, since that's the malt that forms the backbone of Johnnie Walker Gold.

This sort of thing pays off in spades: First, for the bartender, who is recognized as someone who knows what he's doing; next, for the customer, who learns about something new; and also for the boss, who reaps the rewards in the register. Then the bartender gets bigger tips, the customer tells his friends, and the synergy of the whole thing comes together in harmony. It's a beautiful thing.

There's nothing wrong, of course, with trying to turn people on to drinks with which they aren't too familiar, but being mindful of their tastes is usually the best way to go.

Changing the World

Bartenders can change the world. I believe that with all my heart. I'll say it again: Bartenders can change the world. You wanna know how? It's pretty simple, actually.

When a guest come to your bar and she's feeling down, maybe she and her boyfriend just broke up, or perhaps she lost her job, or had a row with a good friend, it's up to you to try to make her feel better. It's your job, providing you have time, of course, to give her a shoulder to cry on, to listen to her problems, and to react from a position of love when you point out that life will go on and she won't feel this way forever. It's your job to be of service to your guest, so that when she leaves your bar she's happier than when she walked in.

If you achieve that, then you are changing the world. That guest will pass that happiness along to the very next person she meets, and it will get paid forward over and over again. Suppose you make ten people feel great on a Thursday night, and they pay that forward to another ten people? And suppose that 50 bartenders in your town do the same thing, and that 50 bartenders in 1,000 towns and cities, in hundreds of countries all over the world do the same thing on the same night? And suppose those same bartenders do that same thing 365 days a year? What will happen then? Well, I think we'll have changed the world.

Go to it.

WHO CAN ABSTAIN ALTOGETHER?

"A man who is drunk is like one struck on the head; his wisdom and skill avail him not at all. Get drunk only three times a month. It would be better not to get drunk at all. But who can abstain altogether?"

Genghis Khan: The Emperor of All Men by Harold Lamb. New York: Garden City Publishing Company, 1927.

Part 3

The Nuts & Bolts of the Bartender's Craft

We took a look at the philosophical side of our craft in the previous chapter, so now it's time to look at how we do our jobs from a physical viewpoint. I'm not a great believer in laying down rules on methodology and I give much leeway to personal style, but there are some aspects of our craft that it's imperative to understand if we want to keep our standards high. Hopefully I've covered much of this in this chapter.

THE GREATEST
ACCOMPLISHMENT
OF A BARTENDER

"The greatest accomplishment of a bartender lies in exactly suiting his customer. This is done by inquiring what kind of a drink he wishes to have and how he desires to have it mixed … In following this rule, the barkeeper will soon gain the esteem and respect of his patrons."

The New and Improved Illustrated Bartenders' Manual or How to Mix Drinks of the Present Style: How to Mix Drinks of the Present Style by Harry Johnson, 1900.

Chapter 1

Methodology

"Sometimes these saloons become so densely thronged that there is much difficulty in elbowing one's way to the 'bar,' where showily-dressed male attendants, conspicuous for jewellery, immaculate linen aprons, and having their shirtsleeves tucked up, perform the occult mysteries of their spiritual office." *Life and Society in America* by Samuel Phillips Day, 1880.

Making a good drink isn't much more than using good ingredients in the correct proportions and mixing them according to the prescribed method, and this certainly isn't rocket science. However, many new methods of mixing, straining, and serving drinks have been born in the past decade, and yet more might have been around for a good long time but they've been known only to bartenders in specific bars until the recent past. Modern-day communications have changed all that, and although the bartender needs to know no more now that he did 10 years ago in order to perform his job, I'm going to try to detail all of these differing styles of methodology so that individual bartenders can choose for themselves which of the various methods suit their styles best. For instance, you might have always stirred your Dry Gin Martinis, but after reading this chapter you could decide to "throw" them, instead. I won't be covering everything in this volume since there just isn't room, so I'll detail more new techniques in each subsequent edition of the *Annual Manual.*

For the most part, my explanations of how to hold a shaker and of some of the details of how to mix drinks should be taken as mere guidelines, since personal style is far more important if you want to be seen as a good bartender. There are some places where safety and science come into play, so please try to take notice of specific instructions on things such as how long to stir or shake a cocktail—something that has been ignored by some younger bartenders in the past few years, and something that really gets my goat. There's a reason that drinks must be shaken or stirred for a certain length of time, and if a bartender doesn't know *why* s/he is doing what s/he's doing, then the bartender doesn't understand the craft. This stuff is very easy to grasp, but if the bartender doesn't take the time to learn why we do what we do, then s/he's lost, I'm afraid. That said, you must feel absolutely free to develop or use your own personal style of actually holding, say, a Boston shaker, just as long as it works well for you and the shaker doesn't become a missile or drink doesn't end up on the floor.

This chapter is dedicated to bartender methodology, with discussions about equipment and ingredients, though ingredients are covered in greater detail in the next chapter. I've tried my level best to cover lots of the new techniques I've seen since I wrote *Joy of Mixology*, but no doubt I've missed a few things here and there. You know how to reach me, right?

I've also tried to not be too very geeky here, so although I believe that I've included as much information as you'll need to do your job well, I haven't used some of the scientific terminology that you'll find on some of the more scientific web sites. I happen to love those sites (Dave Arnold rocks), but I'm just not qualified to bandy those terms around. It's important, I think, to leave that stuff to them as understands it in depth, while every-day working bartenders need know only the essential facts in order to master many twenty-first-century techniques.

Much of what follows, when it comes to classic methodology, has been taken from *The Joy of Mixology*, but I've updated the content, extensively at times, and I've added some comments in various subjects in order to underscore some aspects of the technique in question that I've witnessed being ignored of late. Read carefully, please.

A Word about Measurements

I live in the USA, and in some respects this country can seem to be behind the rest of the world. We still use Imperial measurements, for instance, when the rest of the world is more metrically inclined. I'm told that 1 US fluid ounce = 29.5735296 milliliters, so I'm taking that up a little and all liquid measurements in this book will be given in both milliliters and ounces, using the formula 30 milliliters = 1 US fluid ounce for ease. It ain't precise, but neither are we bartenders for the most part.

Chilling Glasses

Any chilled cocktail that is served without ice should be poured into a pre-chilled glass, and the easiest and best way of achieving this is to keep glasses in the fridge or the freezer. But if you don't have room there, a couple of other methods can be used.

One way to chill a glass is to keep it upturned or buried in a mound of crushed ice, but this is possible only at bars that have an extra sink or space for a suitable receptacle. Ideally the crushed ice will be held in a sink or bowl that is fitted with a drain so that melted ice will not become a problem, but if this is not viable you can use, say, a punch bowl or similar vessel. Be aware that you'll have to drain the bowl periodically, so be sparing with the ice or it will become unmanageable.

The most common method of pre-chilling glasses is to fill them with ice and water and let them sit while you mix the drink. I recommend that whenever possible you stand the glass in a sink and run water into it until it overflows—the water that clings to the outside of the glass will help chill it more quickly. Before pouring the drink you must, of course, empty the glass of the ice and water: Holding it by the base or the stem, shake the glass vigorously for a few seconds, allowing the cold water to spill over the outside of the glass and into the sink, empty it, and then once again shake it vigorously to rid it of any last drops of water. When properly chilled, the glass should be frosted on the outside.

Rimming Glasses

Bartenders have gotten very creative with their rimming ingredients in recent years, but *there are still a few sorry souls out there who coat both the inside and the outside of the rim of the glass*. I hope that you aren't one of them... .

To rim a glass properly, first you must moisten the rim, which can be accomplished in two ways, and you'll need a shallow saucer full of the dry ingredient. The first technique—my favorite—is to take a wedge of an appropriate citrus fruit (lime for a Margarita, lemon for a Sidecar, for instance), and slot the inner fruit side over the rim of the glass. Now, squeezing the fruit gently to release a little juice, slide the wedge around the rim of the glass until the whole perimeter is moist. Hold the glass by the base in one hand, and hold your other hand vertically to form a bridge. Set the glass on the index finger of your "bridge" hand so that the rim faces downward at a 45-degree angle and rests on the surface of the dry ingredient. Using the hand that's holding the base, rotate the glass until the whole rim is coated. Remove any of the dry ingredient that might have stuck to the glass below the rim—you're trying to achieve a straight line, about 1/4-inch deep, around the perimeter of the glass—with a dry cocktail napkin.

The second method is different only inasmuch as, to moisten the rim, you dip the glass into a saucer full of one of the ingredients in the drink. Cointreau, for instance, works well for both the Sidecar and the Margarita. Admittedly, in both methodologies, a little liquid makes its way into the interior of the glass, but the amount is negligible and the alternative is simply too labor intensive to be viable.

If you expect to make large quantities of any drink that calls for a glass with a coated rim, it's best to prepare glasses before your customers or guests arrive, and this is also preferable because, given time to dry thoroughly, the dry ingredient will better adhere to the glass.

Whatever you do, though, don't *ever* upturn a moistened glass into a saucer of the dry ingredient, coating the inside of the rim as well as the outside. I might be watching.

Ingredient Pouring Order

The old rule of thumb about which ingredient should be poured first when making a cocktail or mixed drink was "least expensive leads." The reasoning behind this was that if you made the mistake of pouring too much of any one ingredient, you'd waste less of the expensive stuff. However, this isn't a hard and fast rule. You'd never, for example, pour tonic into a highball glass before adding gin or vodka.

I'm a great believer in always pouring the base ingredient of any drink first. This way you get a *feel* for how much of the other ingredients to pour. If you trust your intuition, you'll innately know how to balance a drink, providing you know your ingredients. It's a mindful thing. Hence, when making a Sidecar, say, I always pour the brandy first, followed by a well-made triple sec like Cointreau or Grand Marnier, and then I add the lemon juice last. It's precisely the opposite of the rule dictated by price. Each to his own, though. I don't believe that this matters too very much.

Pouring

The only guidance I'm giving here about actual pouring is this: If you're pouring from a bottle fitted with a pour-spout, when you hold the bottle, be sure to wrap your index finger or your thumb over the base of the pourer. This is a safety precaution. If a pourer is a little loose, you run the risk of it falling from the bottle, and even if you know that a particular pourer has a tight fit, it's imperative that you make a habit of holding bottles in this fashion so that you never make a mistake.

The way in which bartenders measure their ingredients when pouring is a very personal matter. I prefer to free-pour, but many bartenders insist on using jiggers or other precise measuring devices, and a few prefer to pour by eye. Which way is best? Providing you turn out great drinks consistently, the way that you prefer is best. It's as simple as that. What follows, then, is a series of short discussions about various styles of measuring while pouring.

Pouring by Eye

Precision can be attained when pouring by eye only if you use a glass that you know very well indeed, and you know exactly the point to pour to in that glass to achieve 15 ml (.5-ounce) increments. Measures of 7.5 ml (.25 ounces) and less are guessed for the most part, no matter how precise you think you're being.

Pouring by Jigger

Jiggers and other measuring devices are, of course, very precise, and can be used satisfactorily for most drinks, but I've noticed that very few bartenders use them with any degree of precision at all. They use them as guides rather than exact measures. Free-pouring, when properly administered, is every bit as precise as this.

Free-Pouring

I prefer the very American free-pour system by far. It gives the bartender a chance to show a little flair in his pouring style, and allows him to *feel* his way through a drink. Also, when making drinks that are to be served straight up, there's nothing better than seeing a full Martini glass after the bartender drains every last drop from a shaker or mixing glass, thus showing that precision is part of his craft.

In order to learn how to free-pour you should first practice with a bottle of water fitted with a pourer. Holding the bottle in the prescribed manner, with your thumb or index finger wrapped around the base of the pour-spout, pour water from the bottle into a measuring device such as a 1-ounce jigger, and as you pour, count silently in your head. When the jigger is full, stop pouring and remember how far you got in your counting. Repeat this until you end up at the same number every single time, and from that moment on, that number will be your one-ounce-pour number. Since people count at different rates of speed there's no use telling anyone to count to, say, four, in order to achieve a perfect shot—every bartender should have his own number.

Building Drinks

Drinks such as the Screwdriver, a scotch and soda, or a gin and tonic, which are served in a highball glass, are known as "built" drinks. Although Negronis and various drinks such as the Black Russian are often built in the glass, too, it's preferable to stir them over ice in a mixing glass then strain the drink into a highball glass filled with fresh ice. This way the drink is chilled and diluted before it is served.

To build a highball, simply fill the glass with ice, add the ingredients—liquor first—then stir the drink with a sipstick a few times, add any garnish that's called for, and serve it, complete with the sipstick. If the garnish is a citrus wedge or twist, it should be added before the drink is stirred, but if it's an ornamental garnish such as an orange wheel, stir the drink before adding the garnish.

Most people will stir the drink a few extra times with the sipstick before discarding it and proceeding to drink. Now you have a wet sipstick on your sparkling clean bar—don't let it languish there. Discard it immediately. Some customers, however, insist on keeping their used sipsticks so they know how many drinks they've had, and if this is the case there's not much you can do about it, but you might want to put them on an extra coaster so they don't look quite so untidy.

Layering Drinks

Layered drinks are generically known as Pousse Cafés, and the preparation of these drinks displays the height of showmanship of the bartender. Layering is usually achieved by slowly pouring liqueurs, spirits, and sometimes even cream or fruit juice over the back of a small spoon or a barspoon, so that the liquid falls very gently on top of the previously poured liquid in the glass and rests on top in a new layer. Other objects can be used instead of a spoon, and the first time I witnessed this was in 1993, when New Orleans bartender **Lane Zellman** poured the ingredients for his creation—The AWOL—over a maraschino cherry. He held the cherry by the stem, and the effect was very entertaining.

In order to know which ingredients will float on others you need to know, or at least have an idea of, the density of each component of the drink. However, this can be somewhat difficult since liqueurs are made by many different producers, and depending on the formulas used, the density of one bottling of, say, white crème de menthe is not necessarily the same as another.

Having said that, it can be fairly simple to guess correctly what will float on what, just by knowing the texture of a spirit or liqueur. In general, the more sugar an ingredient has, the denser it will be. Heavy syrups such as grenadine, for instance, will usually withstand the weight of lots of liqueurs and so

101

should be one of the first ingredients added to the glass. Cassis, crème de bananes, crème de menthe, and crème de cacao are also fairly heavy, syrupy liqueurs, so it stands to reason that lighter products such as triple sec, kirsch, and sloe gin will float on any of the above products. Spirits such as brandy, whiskey, rum, tequila, vodka, and gin will usually float on top of many liqueurs since they contain no sugar, and are, therefore, lighter.

Muddling

The term muddling refers to the action of combining ingredients, usually in the bottom of a glass, by pressing down on them, thus grinding them together. This is usually the first step in the making of a drink, and the ingredients being muddled are usually both wet and dry—sugar and bitters, for instance, or mint leaves and simple syrup. You can use a mixing glass, a sturdy old-fashioned glass, or any other glass that's tough enough to withstand the pressure exerted, and you'll need a muddler—essentially a short stick usually made of wood or hard plastic. Muddlers come in lots of different shapes and sizes, and once again, whichever works best for you is the best muddler on the market. Personally I prefer PUG! Muddlers, for a few specific reasons: I prefer using unvarnished wood. I love the way they look. The slanted cut on the hand-held end makes for easy handling. And finally, I love PUG! Muddlers because **Chris Gallagher**, a very good friend of mine, makes them. Catch him at jcgallagher08@hotmail.com. (And don't tell **David "Mr. Mojito" Nepove** that I said that. He makes some fabulous muddlers too. Catch him at mrmojito@mistermojito.com, or visit http://mistermojito.com/.)

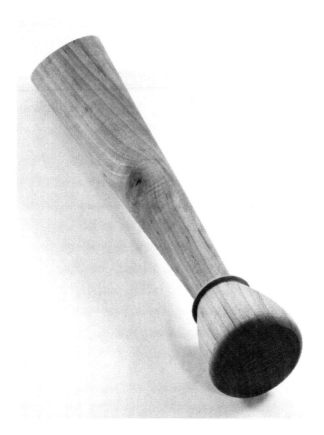

The Old-Fashioned, the Mojito, and the Caipirinha all require muddling, and depending on where you stand on the subject of muddling mint for a Julep, the Mint Julep can fit into this style of drink, too.

You can also muddle lemon wedges with granulated sugar to make a Tom Collins or a Whiskey Sour. The sugar abrades the zest of the lemons and produces a far fresher-tasting drink. This same phenomenon occurs in a Caipirinha, when granulated sugar is muddled along with lime wedges, and if you use simple syrup you can lose that extra sparkle that the sugar brings to the drink.

When sugar is called for as an ingredient to be muddled, some liquid will also be needed in order to dissolve it. Sometimes the liquid comes from the juice of whatever fruit is being muddled, or it might come from a few dashes of bitters. Don't hold back when muddling—squeeze every last drop of juice from fruit wedges by pressing on them firmly and repeatedly with the pestle, and grind the sugar into the liquid until it dissolves completely.

I have witnessed one other form of muddling drinks in just one city, Seattle, and hence have dubbed it the Seattle Muddle, though I'm sure that bartenders in other cities must sometimes use this method of mixing. In order to perform the Seattle Muddle you must first pour all the ingredients of any given cocktail or mixed drink into a mixing glass two-thirds full of ice. Next wrap your hand over the top of the glass, and with the other hand insert the pestle into the glass between your thumb and forefinger. Now, plunge the pestle up and down, mixing the drink thoroughly before straining it into the serving glass.

The Seattle Muddle is a somewhat messy affair and it's slightly unhygienic since the drink splashes against your palm as you mix it, sometimes actually spilling out of the glass if you don't form a watertight seal with your hand. However, this method has the effect of breaking tiny shards off the ice and these morsels will remain in the drink after it has been strained. In the case of a cocktail that's being served straight up, these shards form sparkling little "stars" that float on top of the drink—the visual effect is quite appealing (though I know that some of you hate that!).

Stirring and Shaking: When to Do Which

Most bartenders will agree that, as a generalization: Drinks containing opaque ingredients like fruit juices, cream liqueurs such as Bailey's, eggs, or dairy products such as cream, half and half, or milk, should be shaken, and that clear drinks such as the classic Martini or Manhattan are usually stirred. It's fairly simple to determine why some drinks should be shaken: It's far easier, for instance, to thoroughly combine a spirit with heavy cream or a fruit juice by shaking rather than stirring, whereas drinks made with a spirit and vermouth or other liquid of similar density, such as the Martini or Manhattan, are easily mixed together when stirred.

Some bartenders choose to stray from classical methods as a matter of personal style, and bear in mind, too, that there are exceptions to the rule. Some exceptions include clear drinks such as the Stinger, for instance (brandy and white crème de menthe), which is normally shaken, not stirred. A classic Gin Martini, however, should be stirred, even though some old recipe books prescribe shaking the drink. Some customers will specifically ask for a shaken Martini. Their wish is your command.

Temperature

The temperature of the drink is an important factor to consider when shaking or stirring. Some people think that, by using a metal receptacle such as a cobbler-style cocktail shaker or the metal half of a Boston shaker, the resultant drink is far colder than if you use glass. This is true, but not significantly so. The real key to bringing a drink down to the right temperature is the amount of time you spend stirring or shaking. Shaking requires approximately half as much time in order to reach the correct temperature as does stirring. As a rule of thumb, you should shake a drink for 10 to 15 seconds, or stir it for 20 to 30 seconds.

You might hear some people say that Gin Martinis should be stirred rather than shaken in order to avoid "bruising" the gin, but this is a misconception—gin can't be bruised. It's more than likely that the "bruising" referred to here is, in fact, a chill haze—the cloudiness that can occur when certain items get too cold. Martinis are sometimes made with as much dry vermouth as gin, and when this drink is well chilled, the congeners in the vermouth will develop this haze. There is nothing wrong with a cloudy Martini save for its appearance.

Dilution

When we shake or stir drinks over ice, we are adding an extra ingredient to the cocktail: water that melts from the ice. This, despite what some bar-tweenies have been saying of late, is a desirable thing. Cocktails and mixed drinks should slide down the throat gracefully, and this isn't possible if there's too big of a percentage of alcohol in the glass. I'm the sort of a drinker who likes strong drinks—ask around—but when I build my Manhattan on the rocks of an evening, not bothering to stir it over ice and strain it into a glass filled with fresh ice, it's seldom that I touch the drink for five minutes or so. I keep giving it a quick stir with my dandy antique cocktail stirrer that

I keep in an old metal shot glass by my chair, and eventually I'll start to sip. If it's still too strong, though, I'll be patient, and I'll wait a little longer for the drink to achieve perfect dilution. A 120-ml (4-oz) drink should contain 30 ml (1 oz) of water melted from the ice. Don't let me down on this. The tweenies know not what they say.

Stirring Drinks

Before you prepare a drink that calls for stirring as the prescribed methodology be sure to have a chilled glass, or a glass containing ice cubes if the drink is to be served on the rocks, at the ready. You can stir drinks in the base of a cobbler shaker if you wish, but I prefer, by far, to use the mixing glass half of a Boston shaker. Showmanship is very important when tending bar, and drinkers love to see those ice cubes move up and down and round and round when you prepare their drink in a mixing glass, so this is the receptacle that I recommend above all others.

The standard barspoon has a twisted shaft, and this isn't merely stylistic. It's a functional part of the design. To stir a drink properly, hold the twisted part of the shaft of the spoon between your thumb and first two fingers. Plunge the spoon into the mixing glass, twirl the spoon between your fingers away from, then toward yourself, and simultaneously move the spoon up and down in the glass. Sounds hard but it isn't. That's the way I was taught to hold a spoon back in the 1970s, but many bartenders have perfected far more elegant ways of doing this these days. Even I have changed the way in which I hold the spoon, and the shaft now rests between my second and third fingers as I rotate it in the glass. Suit yerself. Just make it look pretty.

Stir the drink for between 20 and 30 seconds in order to bring the temperature down to the correct temperature and to achieve the right amount of dilution, then strain the drink into the chilled glass.

Shaking Drinks

I haven't changed much about the way I shake drinks. I still prefer to use a Boston shaker, with its simple components—two cones, one metal, one glass—for shaking purposes. There's something about a Boston shaker that makes me think that a bartender means business. It's a serious tool.

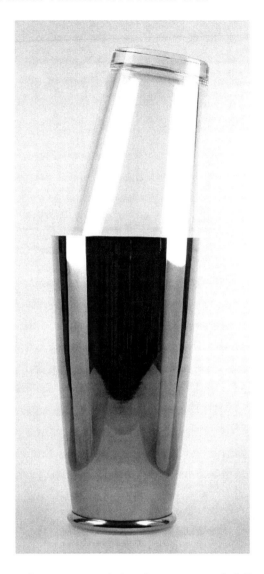

After you have prepared the glassware needed for the cocktail, fill the mixing glass half of the shaker about two-thirds full of ice. Pour in the ingredients for the drink and place the metal half of the shaker on top of the glass, giving it a sharp tap on the base to ensure it has formed a watertight seal. Hold the shaker however it feels most comfortable to you, just as long as you keep the two parts together during shaking *and as long as the glass half of the shaker isn't pointing at anyone.* Sometimes Boston shakers break apart in mid-shake and the glass goes flying through the air. Make sure that if this happens, the glass hits the backbar, not your guest. I heard of one such case in which a customer lost her short-term memory after she was hit by a flying mixing glass.

Make sure that you shake for between 10 to 15 seconds, and then, holding the shaker so that the metal part is on the bottom, tap the metal sharply with the heel of your hand at the point where the two receptacles are joined. This will break the seal and you will be able to lift the glass off the metal container. It's very important to keep the metal on the bottom when breaking the seal—if the glass is on the bottom, sometimes the action of hitting the shaker causes liquid to spill over the lip of the glass, wetting your hand and the glass, and thus causing the glass to slip to the floor. If the metal is on the bottom, this can't happen. If you have a problem breaking the seal with the heel of your hand—and this happens to even the most seasoned professionals—tap the metal sharply at the same place on the edge of the bar or another solid surface. Some people worry that this action could break the glass, and I've seen that happen. I've seen it happen only once in over 40 years, though.

The Hard Shake and the Vicious Shake

Before I get into the Hard Shake and the Vicious Shake, I'm turning you over to **Toby Cecchini** for a discussion of ice and shaking, though I've added my opinion on the subjects after Toby's article.

On the Rocks, It's a New Landscape by Toby Cecchini. Reprinted with permission from The *New York Times*, August 25, 2009:

ONCE upon a time, ice was simply cold and hard. A barkeep would scoop some into a shaker, pour on the spirits, cap it, give it a ride and strain it out, creating one of life's great simple entertainments. But in the current renaissance of cocktail culture, where attention to every facet of the drink has reached the fetishistic, ice has become as fraught a signifier of a bartender's seriousness as the now ubiquitous arm gaiters.

A coterie of young, ambitious mixologists are using enormous cubes custom made by ice sculpture suppliers for shakers, ice balls the size of oranges for drinks on the rocks, long ice tubes for highballs, pea-size ice in frosty swizzles and pieces muddler-crushed in muslin for juleps.

Along with this new compulsion over form, there's a new take on the ice's function. Traditionally as you chilled a drink, you wanted to dilute it, using the melted ice to blend the juices and syrups, to open the aromatics in the liquors and bring it all together harmoniously at a more palatable strength.

The new thinking is that drinks should be kept as strong as possible. Dilution has become a dirty word. This means in a few of the world's more epicurean watering holes you may witness young bartenders shaking drinks without ice or loading in large hand-hewn chunks, with less surface area to melt, then shaking furiously but briefly and "double straining" through fine mesh to remove any rogue ice particles.

The culmination of this ethos is the "martini" at the Dukes Hotel in London, where vermouth is spritzed across a chilled glass from an atomizer and your drink is disgorged directly from a frozen bottle of gin, negating the debate over stirring or shaking.

Shaking styles themselves have also come under new scrutiny, becoming for bartenders the showcase of élan that knife skills are for cooks.

For this, we largely can thank **Kazuo Uyeda**, who's been mixing drinks for four decades in Tokyo, where a bartender can apprentice for six months simply hand-carving ice shapes like diamonds and balls from blocks of ice.

Mr. Uyeda, who owns a bar named **Tender** in the Ginza district, is the inventor of a much-debated shaking technique he calls the hard shake, a choreographed set of motions involving a ferocious snapping of the wrists while holding the shaker slanted and twisting it.

According to his Web site, this imparts, among other things, greater chill and velvety bubbles that keep the harshness of the alcohol from contacting the tongue, while showering fine particles of ice across the drink's surface.

You'll be excused for not knowing who Mr. Uyeda is, but no envelope-pushing bartender within blogshot is without an opinion on the hard shake.

Eben Freeman, the figurehead of molecular mixology at **Tailor**, who is one of few non-Asian adherents of the practice, avows that the hard shake's precision is akin to the Japanese tea ceremony, drawing on aesthetics and precision, and calibrated to a much more refined palate.

"Westerners don't understand the religious philosophy behind Japanese bartending," he said. "The hard shake's true distinction is imparting texture, which is unmeasurable except to the human tongue."

To non-believers, such justification is a new set of clothes for the emperor. Mr. Uyeda seems to be the only practitioner who is acknowledged to perform the hard shake properly.

But even as a cult phenomenon, its influence is undeniable.

In an attempt to shine the unsparing light of science on these issues, **Eben Klemm**, senior manager of wine and spirits for **B.R. Guest** restaurants and a former biotech researcher; **Alex Day**, a bartender at **Death & Co.** in Manhattan; and **Dave Arnold**, the director of culinary technology at the French Culinary Institute, recently presented a seminar at Tales of the Cocktail, an annual convention of all things cocktailian in New Orleans.

They conducted experiments to determine how shakers, sizes of ice and shaking styles affect dilution and chill rates.

To measure these, they rigged cocktail shakers with electronic thermocouples that projected data in graph form onto a screen. Using variations of large hunks, normal cubes and crushed ice, they ran trials shaking a variety of drinks. To the astonishment and embarrassment of more than a few bartenders present, they found effectively no difference for any of the variables.

Across a range of ice sizes and shaking styles that varied from Mr. Day's mannered syncopation to Mr. Arnold's self-described "crazy monkey," all approaches arrived at almost exactly the same temperature and dilution.

What this means for the hard shake is unclear. Its few defenders in the United States claim the New Orleans experiment proves little, as the hard shake is more about the texture it creates than merely chilling and diluting.

"The only thing we couldn't really measure was texture," Mr. Klemm mused. "But I'm coming after that next: aeration levels, weak-ion interactions ..."

Last week, in an initial attempt at a test for texture, Mr. Klemm and Mr. Arnold, with **Audrey Saunders** of the **Pegu Club** and **Nils Norén**, a vice president of the French Culinary Institute, had four bartenders shake identical Daiquirí mixtures. They found the results, judged by taste and the "wash lines" the drinks left at their fluffiest, post-shaking, were surprisingly uniform. But Mr. Arnold acknowledged that his methodology may need refining.

"What's going be left after 'texture,' though, that's the next question," he said. "All this mystic stuff, it's all theater, and that's not to be minimized. Anything that makes you focus on what you're doing can only make you better."

In "The Thin Man," William Powell lectures a group of bartenders on how to shake drinks: "The important thing is the rhythm. Always have rhythm in your shaking. Now a Manhattan you shake to fox-trot time, a Bronx to two-step time, a Dry Martini you always shake to waltz time." Can such intangibles be measured? Gentlemen, start your thermocouples (and your metronomes).

> **gaz sez:** *I started a thread on Diageo's World Class Finals Facebook page on the subject of "Does Size Matter" when it comes to ice cubes, and after much back and forthing with some very knowledgeable people, as well as consulting the wisdom of* **Chef Dave Arnold** *from the French Culinary Institute, these are my conclusions:*

The temperature of ice cubes makes a difference—colder cubes chill faster.

The size of the ice cubes will dictate how long it takes to chill a drink to optimum temperature (whatever you believe that to be). Smaller cubes chill the drink faster.

The size of the ice cubes makes absolutely no difference to the dilution/temperature ratio: If two drinks at the same temperature are poured into two shakers, one containing large cubes, and the other containing small cubes, and if both sizes of ice cubes are at the same temperature, then the drinks will not attain perfect serving temperature without both of them being diluted equally.

And furthermore, cocktails require dilution. A well-made cocktail should be comprised of approximately 75% ingredients, and 25% water melted from ice. Cocktails should be easy to drink—they aren't supposed to be a street brawl in a glass.

Now let's look at the hard shake: I do believe that the hard shake gives a drink a smoother, silkier texture, and I also believe that the exact same texture can be achieved simply by shaking a drink with lots of gusto. Shaking it like you mean it. As far as I'm concerned, the only advantage to the hard shake, with all due respect to Kazuo Uyeda (and **Stan Vadrna**, my brother), is that it's great to watch. It's theater. And tending bar is, to a large degree, performance art, so I believe that the hard shake has merits all its own.

When this topic came up on the Global World Class Facebook page in December, 2010, and with tongue planted firmly in cheek, I came up with the term *vicious shake*: Shaking a drink violently, as if nothing in the world matters more than making the ice cubes run amuk ("mad with uncontrollable rage") within the shaker.

115

I contend that it's impossible to tell the difference between a drink shaken using Mr. Uyeda's hard shake, and a drink that's shaken very viciously—a method that I tend toward. When I mentioned this, again on Diageo's World Class Facebook page, **Kenji Jesse**, the man who roams the earth extolling the virtues of Smirnoff Black Label, chimed in with a quote from Mr. Uyeda that he'd collected after asking: "Is the hard shake just a physical motion of body and shaker or is there a state of mind that one must employ to achieve perfection in its technique?"

Mr. Uyeda's answer: "Technique shows your heart. That means you cannot make a great cocktail if you only do a great hard shake physically. More important is your passion to make the best cocktail you possibly can. I would say, 'If there is no heart, you have no technique.' The heart is much more important to me. In other words, technique is the tool to show your heart. So, heart must come first. Your heart really appears in the cocktail you make in a variety of ways. If making a cocktail is all about technique, then a machine can make the best cocktail. But, in fact, a machine cannot. Bartending is craftsmanship. It is not a digital world, but it is always an analog world with heart and then skill. People have an image of the hard shake as shake hard because of its name. But this is not true. If the hard shake means how hard you can shake physically, I could never top the younger bartenders! The hard shake is about how to make fine air bubbles: how you can break and change the air into the fine air bubble pieces that make cocktails mellow and easy to drink. I think there are many valid hard shake techniques. I have my way, but it is not only the way to do a hard shake. I believe there are as many possible techniques as there are bartenders who do the hard shake. As I have mentioned, the hard shake is not about physical power. Moreover, physical power is an obstacle for the hard shake. The keys are to relax your shoulders and your wrist. I often compare the hard shake to golf. In golf, your lower half of the body has to be stable while your upper body has to relax. You need to let the tension out of the upper body in order to have a fast head speed. Head speed is very important, and to make the fast head speed, you have to loosen up. Loosening up is the point. It is same for the hard shake. You have to create a speed to shake the shaker fast. That means, you need to loosen up your shoulder and wrist to move the shaker faster."

So there you have it, straight from the master's mouth. I'm in awe of Mr. Uyeda. You gotta love a man with so much passion, right?

Dry-Shaking

You may have heard or seen the term "dry shake." This refers to shaking a drink that includes raw eggs, egg yolks, or egg whites without ice. You'll find more information about the dry shake, and other methods of incorporating eggs, in the next chapter. herehere

Rocking and Rolling Drinks

I have heard this method referred to as both rocking and rolling, and it's a way of mixing ingredients without incorporating too much air. **Dale DeGroff**, aka King Cocktail, refers to the method as rolling and suggests that the method is a good one to use when making a Bloody Mary so as to not aerate the tomato juice too much.

To rock or roll a drink, simply combine the ingredients into the glass half of a Boston shaker that is two-thirds full of ice, then pour everything back and forth between the glass and the metal half of the shaker. To thoroughly incorporate the ingredients in a Bloody Mary, this action should be repeated about half a dozen times, ending up with the drink in the mixing glass. Strain the drink into an ice-filled serving glass.

Throwing Drinks

I'm turning this one over to **Robert Hess,** since he has actually visited **Boadas**, the bar in Barcelona where drinks are thrown on a regular basis. This technique is growing in popularity outside of Spain, and I'm not in the least bit surprised since it gives bartenders a chance to show off, and it provides a show for the guests. It's a win/win situation, I think.

Here's what Robert wrote on DrinkBoy.com after he visited Boadas in 2003.

"The night I was there a charming older lady was working behind the bar, I would guess from her dress and attitude, that she was the owner, which I was later to find out was the case. She was **Maria Dolores Boadas** who is Miguel Boadas' [the bar's founder] daughter. She can often be seen working behind the bar mixing up a mean Martini with a unique and entertaining flair that I haven't (yet) seen used elsewhere. The process begins with combining the ingredients, along with ice, in a large cocktail pitcher. After a few quick stirs, they then place a julep strainer over the top and with a long arching motion roll the contents into a pint glass that they hold in the other hand (similar in style to how a Blue Blazer is done). They then pour the contents of the pint glass back in to the pitcher, and then perform another long roll into the pint glass. They do this three or four time, and then strain the drink into your glass."

Okay, if that's the way they do it at Boadas, then that's the way it's done, though I've seen bartenders use different vessels than a cocktail pitcher. Italian bartender **Max LaRocca**, for instance, uses a teapot. He's a good lad, is Max.

Straining Drinks

Although cobbler shakers are fitted with their own strainers, I'm far more enamored of using a spring-loaded Hawthorne strainer or a standard Julep strainer in tandem with a Boston shaker when straining drinks.

Traditionally, the Hawthorne strainer is used when pouring from the metal half of the shaker and the Julep strainer to strain drinks from the mixing glass. After preparing a cocktail, simply fit the strainer firmly over the metal or glass, put your index finger over the top of it to hold it firmly in place, and strain the drink into the serving glass. As you reach the end of the liquid, give the glass a sharp twist in any direction as you return it to an upright position, so that any remaining drops of liquid don't fall to the bartop as you remove the mixing glass.

Fine-Straining or Double-Straining

It's not uncommon to see bartenders straining drinks from the ice into the serving glass using a Hawthorne or Julep strainer as well as through a fine-mesh strainer, thus making sure that absolutely no solids, such as pulp from fruit juice or tiny shards of ice, make their way into the glass. I happen to like seeing fine shards of ice sparkling on top of a cocktail, and I laugh at anyone who tries to tell me that when they melt they will dilute the drink discernibly, but I'll fight to the death for the right of each and every bartender to make her own decision about this matter.

I do ask, though, that you think about why you are fine-straining a drink. I've seen bartenders fine-straining clear drinks such as a Dry Gin Martini that has been stirred, not shaken. That's just plain silly, I think.

Show-Off Straining

If you want to be show-y (and who among us doesn't?!), you can strain drinks into a glass from a height, and this, even for me—I'm very clumsy—isn't very hard to do if you remember that the hand holding the serving glass moves downward, far more than the hand holding the mixing glass moves upwards. Start straining, then, holding the mixing glass directly over the cocktail glass, and hold them at just below shoulder level. As you start to strain, lower the glass a lot, and perhaps move the straining arm upwards just a little. If you've never done this, you'll be surprised at how easy it can be.

Some bartenders strain shaken drinks by holding a complete Boston shaker horizontally over the glass after "breaking" the two parts, a method similar to one used by bartender William Schmidt in the 1890s, but instead of using a shaker, he put one goblet on top of another and "turned them upside down five or six times," held them up together as high as he could with both hands, and let the liquid drip down into a "tall, fancy glass." When using a Boston shaker for this maneuver, the shaker halves are pulled apart slightly so that the liquid pours from the broken seal. I like the showmanship involved in this procedure but recommend that, if you want to adopt that style, you practice with water until you have mastered the maneuver.

Blending Drinks

You might think that making a frozen drink in a blender is a comparatively easy affair, but it's a little more troublesome than you might imagine if you want the resultant drink to be as smooth as silk and sippable through a straw. If you don't have a frozen drink machine at hand you'll have to use a blender to make these. It's best to buy a sturdy commercial blender with a strong motor, since crushing ice places a lot of stress on the machine.

After adding ice and the drink ingredients to the blender glass, set the lid in place and run the blender on high speed (many commercial blenders have only one speed—fast) for 20 to 30 seconds. Turn the blender off, wait until you are sure that the blades are stationary, then remove the lid and thoroughly stir the ingredients with a barspoon. Return the lid to the glass, start the motor again, and repeat the procedure. You might have to stir the drink more than once in order to achieve a perfect frozen drink, but the results are very worthwhile.

You should also use your ears when blending frozen drinks. You'll note that the sound of the motor changes as the ice is crushed and incorporated into the drink. That's when it's time to turn off the motor and check the drink's consistency.

The amount of ice needed to make any specific frozen drink is in direct relationship with the size of the serving glass, so if you aren't sure how much to use, simply build the drink in the glass and then pour the whole thing into the blender. You'll find that this results in a full glass with a slightly convex dome, which is visually appealing.

If you use fruit such as pineapple, peaches, or strawberries in a frozen drink, cut it into manageable pieces before adding the fruit to the blender. In the case of strawberries, hull them and cut them in half; pineapples, peaches, and any similar fruits should be cut into 1-inch cubes. Of course, the pit must be removed from stone fruits, and you shouldn't use the core of a fresh pineapple.

Flaming Drinks

Be careful. Be *very* careful. Flaming drinks can be a hazardous affair at best. Once ignited, if that drink spills you have a fire on your hands, and if it spills onto a person you might have a human torch in the bar. You should *always* have a working fire extinguisher on hand when making flaming drinks, and make damn sure that you know how to use it before you show off your pyrotechnical skills.

But a raging fire isn't all you have to worry about when you make these drinks. If a drink is allowed to flame for too long, the rim of the glass will become very hot and it will stay that way for quite some time. You must warn anybody who insists on a flaming drink of this danger and advise her not to bring the drink to her lips until she can touch the rim of the glass with her finger, and keep her finger there without it being burned.

A few different kinds of drinks can be flamed before service. Straight liqueurs such as Sambuca, for instance, are often flamed, and sometimes the top layer of a Pousse Café is set alight. Other drinks that have, say, a high-proof spirit such as 151-proof rum floated on top can also be ignited to impress customers.

To flame drinks such as these, simply touch a lighted match to the surface of the drink until it catches fire. Allow it to burn for approximately 10 seconds before extinguishing it by placing a small saucer on top of the glass. The bartender should never blow out the flame on a customer's drink—it's unsanitary behavior and I'll slap your wrist if I catch you doing that.

Serving Drinks

Never fill cocktail glasses to the rim. Never. Are you listening? Why would you want to put your guest in the position of trying to get the darned thing to his mouth without spilling? And if the drink is being made for a customer at a table, the waitperson must deliver it without the drink spilling over the side of the glass, which results in a sloppy mess on the serving tray as well as some pretty sticky fingers for both the server and the customer.

All drinks should be served in sparkling clean glasses on a coaster or a napkin that will absorb condensation. Coasters should also be provided for beer bottles if the whole bottle doesn't fit into the glass, or if the customer wishes to pour it himself.

Drinks are normally prepared in the small trough on the bartender's side of the bar and then placed in front of the customer, but sometimes a drink such as a Martini straight up is strained into a glass that already has been placed in front of the customer. It's very important that the customer is able to see you prepare their drink, so don't assemble it out of his view. Ideally, you should stand directly in front of the customer whose drink you are making, and make sure that he is able to see the label on any bottles you use either before you start to pour, or as you are pouring. This way the customer knows that he is getting what he asked for, and he will also enjoy the show as you mix the drink.

If drinks contain sipsticks or other inedible garnishes—plastic mermaids and the like—watch to see when the customer removes these from his drink and sets them down on the bar, and then remove then immediately. You should also watch to see when coasters and napkins become wet because of condensation from the glass, or a customer spilling his drink when picking it up. Remove the offending coaster and replace it immediately.

TO BE A SALOON-KEEPER
AND KILL A MAN WAS TO BE
ILLUSTRIOUS

"I am not sure but that the saloon-keeper held a shade higher rank than any other member of society. His opinion had weight. It was his privilege to say how the elections should go. No great movement could succeed without the countenance and direction of the saloon-keepers ... To be a saloon-keeper and kill a man was to be illustrious."

Roughing It by Mark Twain, 1871.

Chapter 2

Ingredients & Garnishes Focus, 2011

I'll focus on different ingredients and garnishes in each *Annual Manual*, and in this volume I'm kicking it off with eggs and citrus, bringing you some basic information on lime and lemon wedges *that some young whippersnappers out there still haven't learned*, moving on to twists, flaming twists, and how to deal with both in a manner that actually results in a better drink. Then we'll look at some basic information about fruit wedges, followed by a very interesting look at fresh fruit juice from **Katy Gerwin**, and we'll end this chapter with a look at bitters, how to make 'em, and why you might not want to bother.

Eggs

Are you afraid of eggs? Thought not. And eggs can bring so much to a drink. A Pisco Sour isn't a Pisco Sour without that silky texture that only raw egg-white can impart to a drink, and without whole eggs there'd be no Tom and Jerry, right? I don't want to live in a world where there's no Tom and Jerry. Let's be sensible about our eggy-wegs, though. Let's learn the right ways to use them, then we can go full-steam ahead and impress our guests with both knowledge and with fabulous eggy-drinks.

Using Eggs in Cocktails

When you're trying to incorporate egg whites, yolks, or whole eggs into a drink, you're going to have to work a little harder to get the correct texture in said drink. In order to cause all the ingredients to come together as one (commonly referred to as emulsification), you can use a few techniques and tools.

One method is known as the *dry shake*. Add the egg and any other ingredients to the shaker and shake the drink *without ice* for five to 10 seconds, and you should be shaking like you mean it, too. Put some effort into this if you want the right results. (And then add ice and shake for an additional 10 to 15 seconds.) This works simply because eggs emulsify more readily at room temperature than they do when chilled. This is a fairly new technique behind the bar (I first saw it circa 2005, when **Chad Solomon** of cuffsandbuttons.com introduced me to this methodology at Cocktails in the Country), and you can apply it to any recipe that calls for eggs, whether it's called for in the instructions or not.

Some bartenders remove the stainless-steel coil from a Hawthorne strainer and drop it into the shaker when they're dry-shaking, and this seems to have the effect of whisking the eggs as well as shaking them, thus helping emulsify the eggs faster.

You can also use a milk frother—one of those electric or battery-operated hand-held devices used by baristas to foam milk for cappuccinos and the like—to properly emulsify drinks containing eggs, and once again, you would use this before adding ice to the shaker. This innovation, we think, came originally from **Jamie Boudreau**, the Seattle-based Canadian who is well known for his creative genius.

I've seen bartenders use a whisk, too, to achieve the same results, and I must say that the bartender who did this, a certain Frenchman by the name of **Maxime Hoerth**, did it with much style and looked oh-so-French as he whipped up the drink in a small mixing bowl in Athens during Diageo's World Class Bartender Finals in 2010. He then transferred the drink to a shaker to chill and strain.

Raw eggs, if you choose to use them, should be cracked into a receptacle other than the mixing glass and checked for freshness, by making sure they don't smell like, well, rotten eggs, before being added to the drink. You can also test whole eggs for freshness before you crack them by putting them in water—if they float, or even if they stand sort of upright rather than lying flat on the bottom of the bowl or pan, they're old.

Salmonella

Egg whites, when handled properly, bring a fabulous silky texture to a cocktail that just can't be otherwise attained, but some people worry about raw eggs causing salmonella poisoning.

An article in the *San Francisco Chronicle*, 2008, by **Cindy Lee**, quotes **George Chang**, food microbiologist and professor emeritus at UC Berkeley, as saying, "In studies of clean, intact eggs from modern egg factory facilities, less than 1 percent of the eggs contain detectable salmonella," and that the risk of salmonella poisoning from eggs is "perhaps even lower than the risk of eating raw salads." And the piece goes on to say that the risk is even smaller with egg whites and quotes **Lawrence Pong**, principal health inspector and manager of food-borne illness outbreak investigations for the Department of Public Health in San Francisco: "Egg whites are alkaline in nature, and salmonella colonies cannot survive there."

Raw Egg Stench

Some folks can't stand the odor that sometimes accompanies raw eggs, and The Chief (**Jon Bonné**, my editor at the *San Francisco Chronicle*), advised me that a drop or two of bitters can mask this unpleasantness quite handily. At the time of writing this I believe that The Chief was experimenting with a Margarita with raw egg white and orange bitters. **Hannah Lanfear**, a bartender friend of mine in London, told me that she uses citrus twists to mask any unpleasant odors in her sours. And you can also combat egg stench by flavoring them prior to use. If you're planning on making some Ramos Gin Fizzes, for instance, you might think about flavoring your eggs with orange zests.

Flavoring Eggs

Robert Wood, bar manager at the **Kenilworth Hotel** in Warwickshire, England, and **Adam Elmegirab**, Aberdeen-based bartender and bitters producer, both advised me about flavoring eggs. Because of their porous shells, eggs are easy to flavor simply by storing them in herbs or teas, or by covering them with lemon twists, for instance. You'll detect the lemon flavors after just one overnight stay in a lemon-twist motel. And I also learned from **Fred Yarm** on http://cocktailvirgin. blogspot.com, that covering eggs with a cloth soaked in, say, lemon oil, can work well to add flavor.

Adam thinks that the practice might have originated in Italy, using truffles to flavor eggs, and this is something that, according to Robert, you can find at **Moto**, the Chicago restaurant famous for its molecular gastronomy.

Citrus Stuff

This section deals with citrus twists, citrus wedges, and lime juice. It's the kind of section that bartenders who have worked behind the stick for six to 12 months might skip, and bartenders who have plied their trade for 10 years or more will probably pore through in case they find something new. Which are you?

Orange and Lemon Twists: Basics

Citrus twists can be cut in many different ways, but in my opinion, bigger is better. The essential oils in a twist are what add flavor to the cocktails they garnish, so the larger the twist, the more oils will be added to the drink.

To prepare citrus twists, remove the stem end of the fruit in order to give it a base, stand it on its base, and carefully cut strips of the zest, or colored outer layer of peel, from the fruit, running your knife from top to bottom. Some of the white inner pith must remain on the twist so that it will be sturdy enough to use properly, but you should make sure that you never cut into the inner pulp of the fruit. The length of each twist, once again, depends on the size of the fruit, but cutting them as long as is possible is always the way to go. The width of

133

the twist will depend on the size and shape of the fruit you are using, but try for as wide as possible in each case.

You can also use a zester to cut citrus spirals, and if you cut twists this way, it's best to cut them at the time of service, holding the fruit above the drink as you work, so that the oils fall onto the drink as they are released. These spirals are decorative, and it's nigh-on impossible to release more oils from them once they've been cut.

When you garnish a drink with a citrus twist, use both hands to hold the twist by the ends between your thumbs and forefingers, then "twist" in opposite directions to releasing the essential oils from the zest onto the top of the drink. The next part is optional, but I also love to rub the colored side of the twist around the rim of the glass so that any remaining oils are left there, and then I drop the garnish into the drink.

A Twist on Twists

Some bartenders have taken to using more than one twist, and releasing the oils from the extras onto the exterior of the glass so that they get onto the guest's fingers and linger there for a good long time. I learned this from **Ricardo Albrecht**, the German finalist at Diageo's World Class competition in London, 2009.

Flaming Twists

If you seek to flame the oils from a twist, thus adding a little pyrotechnical flare to your performance, a little practice will probably be necessary. First of all, when you cut the twist from the fruit you should make it as wide as possible—larger fruits such as oranges are best suited to this maneuver since it's fairly easy to cut a twist from them that's almost one-inch-wide. If you warm the twist a little before squeezing it, you'll stimulate the oils, making them easier to release. Now, have the twist close at hand as you light a match, and hold the match close to the top of the drink. Take the twist in your other hand and hold it by the short sides between your thumb and first two or three fingers, depending on the length of the twist. The colored side of the twist should, of course, be pointing toward the drink. Now hold the twist about an inch or two away from the top of the flame, and squeeze it to release its oils. You will see them sparkle as they leap through the flame onto the top of the drink.

This is a maneuver that works best for most bartenders by employing a match, rather than a lighter. I've seen so many bartenders try to do this with a lighter, holding the flame over the center of the drink, burning their thumb, jumping back, and expressing the oils all over the place. Anywhere other than through the flame and onto the drink.

The only person I've ever seen using a lighter effectively to flame twists has been **Jamie Boudreau**, the transplanted Canadian who holds forth in Seattle. I'm quite sure that there are many other bartenders out there who know how to pull this off, but thus far, Jamie has been the only guy I've witnessed. He holds the lighter vertically at the side of the glass and aims the twist, at about a 45-degree angle, so that the oils shoot through the flame and land on top of the drink. If you don't do it this way, I urge you to use a match instead of a lighter.

Lime and Lemon Wedges: Basics

Lemon and lime wedges are ingredients. Got it? They are used to flavor a drink, not just to make it look pretty. Don't make me take off my earrings. You know how I get about this sort of stuff.

I like to use large wedges of both of these fruits, and although it depends on the size of the fruit, most limes don't yield much more than four wedges, or six at the very most. Lemons will normally yield six to eight viable wedges.

To prepare lemon and lime wedges, first remove both ends of the fruit with a sharp paring knife, then slice the fruit in half vertically or horizontally, depending on the style of wedge you prefer, and then cut each half into equal-sized wedges. Remember that size matters and you need to end up with a wedge large enough to yield about 7.5 ml (.25 oz) of juice—a rule of thumb is that one-quarter of one lime and one-sixth of one lemon should each contain about 7.5 ml (.25 oz) of juice.

I've seen many a bartender send out gin and tonics with the lime wedge hanging onto the rim of the glass so that the customer has to squeeze it herself if she wants some lime juice in there. "But not everyone wants the lime to be squeezed," say some of these so-called professionals. Believe me, customers who don't want the lime wedge to be squeezed will know to order their G & T that way specifically.

So, from now on, *when you add a wedge of lime or lemon to a drink, squeeze the darned thing by holding it between your thumb and forefinger directly above the drink with one hand and cupping your other hand over the far side of the glass to shield your guest's face from any stray squirts of juice.* Now drop the squeezed wedge into the drink, add a sipstick, and stir the drink briefly to incorporate the juice.

Lime Juice: Squeeze on Demand, or Pre-Squeeze Prior to Service?

I head up the "Legendary Bars and Bartenders" department on Drinkology.com, the Pernod-Ricard bartender community site, and we get some interesting discussions going on there. In October, 2010, **Katy Gerwin**, opened a debate about fresh versus pre-squeezed juice. Katy is co-owner with her husband, **Josh**, of the **Casa Vieja Restaurant and Curbside Café** in Corrales, New Mexico, where they go through a lot of lime juice.

After a few back-and-forths between Katy, a few other bartenders, and myself, she decided to conduct an experiment at her restaurant, and she came up with some interesting results. Katy used both a Mexican elbow-style of juicer and a Cuisinart food processor fitted with a juicer attachment, and she tested juices that were a few hours old against freshly-squeezed juice. Here are her results:

"Today at 1:30 pm I hand-squeezed 10 limes and I juiced 10 limes with the Cuisinart juicer. I put them in the walk-in. At 5:30 pm I hand-squeezed another 10 limes and juiced another 10 limes with the Cuisinart juicer. I did not see a huge difference in the yield—if you hand-squeeze properly, you are not losing product, at least not product you would want. We did two tastings with 14 people in each tasting, including chefs, wine reps, restaurateurs, etc. One was a tasting of all four juices, straight. The second was all four juices mixed with water and simple syrup.

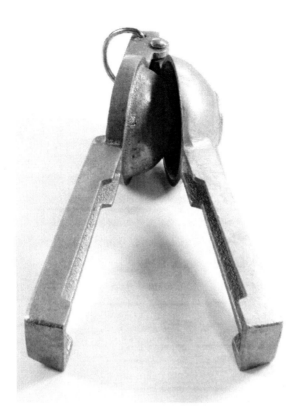

"The overwhelming result was that, above all other things, hand-juicing turned out to be the most important factor. Throw away your [electric] juicer now! Seriously, the difference was AMAZING.

"Secondly, the four-hour-old, hand-pressed juice won by over 72 percent of the votes. Older, or as I prefer to now call it, *settled* juice, tastes better. It has more lime flavor and less acidic bite. Don't misunderstand me—the acid levels are the same. There is plenty of acid in the old juice, it's just more balanced. As a former avid proponent of fresh-squeezed juice, let me say I am shocked. REALLY SHOCKED!! But, it's the truth and the blind tasting shows it.

139

"We have not given up on the hand-squeezing all together. The show is still there. We hand-squeeze all our lemons and oranges to order. The limes are pre-squeezed before the shifts begin. We don't feel we use enough lemon and orange juice to pre-squeeze, just lime."

> **gaz sez:** *I've never met Katy, and it's only recently that she's come to my attention. She's so darned passionate, and she and her husband go to extraordinary lengths both to differentiate themselves, their drinks, and their restaurant, and also to make sure they get things right. This experiment serves to show us such passion, and Katy, like a true bartender, was eager to share it with the world.*

Bitters

In the early 1990s, when Angostura and Peychaud's were almost the only bitters that were readily available and Peychaud's could prove hard to find if you didn't live in a big city, I ran out of orange bitters. If memory serves, I'd stolen a few bottles of De Kuyper orange bitters from some bar or other and I'd used them up during the writing of *The Bartender's Bible*. Fee Brothers orange bitters was available, but I didn't know about that fine company at the time, and we were sorely lacking in search engines back then, so my only option was to make my own. It was a bit of a lark. An adventure. Something that sounded like it might be fun.

I found a recipe for orange bitters in *The Gentleman's Companion: An Exotic Drinking Book*, by Charles H. Baker, Jr., the well-traveled bon-vivant who detailed his trips to various countries and bars around the world, reporting on the drinks he sipped and the people he met. His recipe called for orange peel, cardamom, caraway, and coriander, and it also supplied me with the methodology required to make the stuff, so I set off to the Village to procure the ingredients. I also had to make a run into Connecticut to get hold of some grain alcohol which, for some stupid reason, can't be sold legally in New York.

Strolling around a store that supplies witches, warlocks, and gremlins with the items necessary for their potions and what-not, I found everything I needed to make Baker's formula, and I added some gentian, cinchona, and quassia to the mix for good measure. Give it a little depth, I thought.

Every weekend I played around with these weird and wonderful ingredients. I was working at the North Star Pub in the South Street Seaport at the time, and in my off hours I tended to the jars filled with differing amounts of ingredients that littered the apartment, picking them up, shaking them, checking the color, and occasionally dipping my finger in them to see how they were progressing.

It took a while, but on the fourth try, I came up with a formula that worked well. Very well, in fact. The recipe was published in *The Book of Bourbon*, and I kept **Dale DeGroff** supplied with the stuff at **The Rainbow Room** for a few years, too.

It took about a year to use up the first batch of Regans' Orange Bitters No. 4, and when I made a second batch I realized I'd screwed up big time. They were as bitter as all hell. Had to add tons and tons of caramel before they were palatable.

It might seem logical that bitters are supposed to be bitter, but most bitters are, in fact, sweet. Sure, they have a bitter component, but by and large they are sweet in nature and multifaceted in structure. If bitters are too bitter, then they take attention away from a drink, and that is not their purpose. Where had I gone wrong?

It probably had something to do with the freshness or the intensity of the cinchona, but whatever it was, I knew I had to work on this recipe some more. Enter **Mark Brown**, president and C.E.O. of The Sazerac Company of New Orleans—the same outfit that brings us Peychaud's Bitters. I bumped into Mark, a fine guy if ever there was one, at the Bourbon Festival, and I asked him if he might be interested in working with me to develop a commercial brand of orange bitters. Mark's always up for a wheeze, so after he thought about it for a few seconds he said, "Sure, let's give it a go." Mark is such a wag.

Now the boffins at Sazerac entered the picture. A team of scientist types headed by the wonderful **Stanley Schwam**, who came out of retirement for this particular project, set to work on the recipe, and it wasn't too long before we had a product we all liked. The TTB (Tax & Trade Bureau) liked it too. We sent them a sample for their approval, and they wrote back saying that the bitters were so darned good that they were refusing to let us release them. Seems they weren't bitter enough. The TTB can be like that.

The thing about bitters is that they're classified as "non-potable" alcohol. This means that nobody is likely to swig back a shot or two of the product, even though a couple of dashes in a mixed drink renders the cocktail eminently potable. Apparently the team at the TTB swigged a few shots of our bitters and liked them immensely, so it was back to the drawing board for Stanley's team. They had to make the bitters taste really really bad so that we could sell them. Sounds strange, huh? True, though.

On the sixth attempt, the Sazerac people produced some orange bitters that suited our palates for cocktailian purposes and were sufficiently vile to satisfy the TTB. Regans' Orange Bitters No. 6 was born.

These days, everyone and their handmaidens have their own brands and flavors of bitters, and many bartenders make their own bitters, too, so there are some drinks out there that can be sampled only at the bar where the creator of the bitters works. And although some terrific new bottlings have sprung up in recent years and the vast majority of the ones I've tried have been pretty fabulous, not all of the new commercial bitters are great, I'm sorry to say. Rather than bash specific products here, I'll just say a few words about the purpose of bitters in cocktails and mixed drinks.

143

Bitters add complexity to a drink, and they also serve to bring the other ingredients together in harmony. Don't ask me how that works. It's one of the great mysteries of the universe. When bitters become the star role in a cocktail, though, they devolve the drink into a product that's far less than the sum of its ingredients. I've sampled some bitters, for instance, that, no matter how little are added to a drink, are the first thing I taste when the cocktail hits my tongue.

Try to remember, then, that if you make your own bitters, and they just don't seem to pull off what you'd intended, then that doesn't make you a bad bartender. Just as some chefs make their own veal reduction and others buy it, so some bartenders, who don't have time, inclination, or specialty skills in this area buy their bitters from reputable manufacturers. Bartenders who don't make their own bitters often shine in other areas, and that's where they are best off directing their energies.

And if you'd like to make some bitters using other folks' recipes, I highly recommend that you try the following formula:

Hess' House Bitters

Adapted from a recipe by
Robert Hess,
Seattle, WA.

1 750-ml bottle rye whiskey

2 teaspoons dried gentian

1/2 cup fresh ginger (julienned)

2 tablespoons whole cloves

2 1/2 tablespoons cardamom pods (cracked)

7 whole star anise

7 cinnamon sticks

200 g (1 cup) granulated sugar

Combine all the ingredients except for the sugar in a large jar and store for two weeks, shaking the jar each day. Strain the mixture through cheesecloth. Save both solids and liquid. Add the solids to 3 cups of water in a saucepan. Bring to a boil, reduce the heat, and simmer for half an hour. Strain the mixture and save the water (you can throw out the solids). Put the sugar into a dry Teflon skillet. On medium heat, gently heat the sugar until it just melts. It will turn brown, and get just slightly burnt. Allow the sugar to cool to almost room temperature, or until it is safe to handle Remove the sugar from the skillet and place into a saucepan with the water. Bring to a boil, and then simmer until the sugar is dissolved. Allow to cool completely, and then add the alcohol mixture. Bottle for storage.

AN ABILITY TO UNDERSTAND

"Almost anyone can learn to mix drinks accurately and fast. That is the least of it. I have always believed success behind the bar comes from an ability to understand the man or woman I am serving, to enter into his joys or woes, make him feel the need of me as a person rather than a servant."

This Must be the Place: Memoirs of Jimmie the Barman, by Morrill Cody, 1937.

Other People's Stuff

With a nod to Stuffy Shmitt's album of the same name, and a wink to Martha, my editor, who came up with the idea of using *Other People's Stuff* as the title to this section, I'm now turning the rest of this book over to yous guys.

This section is dedicated to saluting the best of the best bartenders out there, and I've picked them for myriad various reasons, as you're about to discover. Here you'll discover the craft's most innovative bartenders, the people who work behind the stick for all the right reasons, the philanthropists out there, and the world's most creative cocktailians. Keep up the good work. You continue to inspire me on a very regular basis.

THE FIRST INSTRUMENT
OF HIS DESTRUCTION

"Along with other Vanishing Americans is
our friend the old time barkeeper with the
immaculate white apron and the friendly
smile as he asked, 'What's yours, gents.'
… As long ago as the middle [Eighteen-]
Eighties the decline and fall of this wholly
native and admirable artist was forecast by
the auguries of the brass rail. With unerr-
ing vision they recognized, in the coming
of the Cash Register, the first instrument of
his destruction. Its tinkling bell, merry as
a wedding chime on the ear of the saloon
keeper, smote that of his white jacketed
servitor as did the knell that summoned the
condemned to the block on Tower Hill."

Valentine's Manual of Old New York by
Henry Collins Brown, 1927.

Chapter 1

Fabulous Bartender Awards

This is early days, and I'm quite aware that I'm not shouting out to everyone who deserves mention in this volume. But there are many more volumes of the *Annual Manual* to come, and God willing I'll live long enough to cover everyone whose name needs to be preserved to let our brother and sister bartenders a hundred years hence know what was going down in this, The Second Golden Age of the Cocktailian Craft.

I've chosen 12 Fabulous Bartenders, and I've chosen them for many different reasons. I'm shouting out some bartenders because they are truly creative, some because they've been relentless in pushing the envelope, entering and winning competitions and bringing respectability to our craft, and I've chosen some bartenders because they are philanthropic, or because they show the right attitude, care about their guests, and are mindful in their approach to the job.

Here, then, in alphabetical order by each bartender's first name, are the winners of the first annual Fabulous Bartender Awards:

Andy Wells, Atlantic City, NJ.

Andy is the head bartender at Atlantic City's **Ducktown Tavern**. He has 21 years of bartending and beverage management experience, he's an expert in customer care, and he's a writer who has published staff training manuals and journals as well as magazine articles for South Jersey's *Boardwalk Journal*. He owns the Atlantic City Bartender Training Center, is a certified TIPS trainer, and he's head of the board and the creator of the Atlantic City Bartenders' Ball, an event that raises money to support the "HERO" campaign, a federally registered, 501 (c) 3 nonprofit organization dedicated to preventing drunken driving tragedies by promoting the use of safe and sober designated drivers. Andy has won "Top Bartender" and "Best Drink Menus" awards given by the Atlantic City *Weekly*, and he's a five-time nominee for the "Top 40 under 40" list of entrepreneurs in Atlantic County. Phew!

The reason I picked Andy for a Fabulous Bartender Award wasn't because of any of the above. I picked him because of the following quote by him that I found on the pressofatlanticcity.com web site:

"I care about my customers, just like so many other bartenders do. I don't want to get rich all at once. If they get mad at me and don't tip me if I cut them off, but they are safe for the night, I am OK with that."

Congratulations, Andy! You're one hell of a bartender.

I'm giving Andy some space here to tell his story:

"When I started my bartending school I had to make sure that I teach how to be a responsible server. I am a TIPS trainer and try to tell real stories so that they can relate. Unfortunately anytime our great lawmakers try to force us to do something, it gets watered down with the programs they put in place for us to learn, which are taught by someone who might have never served a drink. I'm sure they believe what they are teaching and honestly would want us to listen but, if you know bartenders, we tend to listen with a deaf ear. I felt that if one of our peers or a 'normal' person tried to help, then more of 'us' might listen. So I decided to try to be that person.

"When I was a kid it wasn't easy. Both of my parents were alcoholics and unfortunately they drove us while they were intoxicated. I can remember as if it were yesterday. My mother had been drinking and was too proud to call a cab. Needless to say, she wound up hitting a big dirt mound because my mom didn't see the stop sign that she ran. I wound up under the dashboard and promised myself that I would never be in that spot again [and that I would] try to help prevent it happening to others. Most people who grew up

similarly to me know this story or may have much more horrifying stories to tell.

"When I thought of the Atlantic City's Bartender's Ball I wanted to show the community that the people in the service industry care about our patrons. The HERO campaign was a perfect fit... .

"I have noticed from time to time that when I tell someone that I am a bartender they continue to ask what else I do. I will be the first to admit that yes, being a bartender isn't rocket science or I'm not busting my back at a 9 to 5 job, but I do love what I do and I take it seriously. I have tried the real world of work and I don't know if I would be able to do anything so repetitious. But bartending gives me freedom to be on stage and to have fun while chasing the proverbial buck. So after all the good times behind the bar I thought it was time for me to put up or shut up and to finally make good on that promise I had made to myself under that dashboard." Andy Wells.

Anthony DeSerio,
Old Saybrook, CT.

Anthony DeSerio works at the **Aspen** restaurant in Old Saybrook, Connecticut, and he sent me message via Facebook after he'd been asked by a customer to make a Pimm's Cup "the proper way." "What's the proper way?" I asked him.

Yes, I know how to make a traditional Pimm's Cup, but I was interested to hear what Anthony's take on the subject was. I was delighted to hear that, when he grabbed a cucumber to make the garnish, he overheard the customer say, "he is going to crush it up with the oranges," so he did just that.

"I just went by the customer's indirect directions," he wrote. "I watched her take that first sip and she said that it was just like her dad made them in England. Then she had two more … It felt good to make someone's day."

This, I think, is a great example of what the bartender's job is all about. Anthony didn't let his ego get in the way of pleasing his customer. Rather than make her a classic Pimm's Cup with club soda and a cucumber garnish, he made it the "proper" way according to her wishes. But the real reason I selected him to be on this list is for the following quote: "If your eye is on the tip jar, your back is to the customer." Pretty sweet, huh?

Chad Doll,
Milwaukee WI.

Chad Doll works at **Bryant's Cocktail Lounge** in Milwaukee. He's a bartender after my own heart. Here's the quote that got Chad a place in this year's Fabulous Bartender list:

"I am a bartender, not a bar-chef, not a chef, not a mixologist, not a stir-mix-a-lot ... I take all aspects of my job very seriously, and mixing or creating cocktails falls third in the list of my

job priorities, right behind service and maintaining a comfortable environment for the patrons. I will not laugh or make you feel like an idiot if you want a apple or chocolate Martini, flavored vodka and Sprite, or a fist bump delivered with your Jager Bomb." Chad Doll.

Duggan McDonnell, San Francisco, CA.

I've known Duggan for quite a few years, and he and I get along like a house on fire when we're out on the town. The following quote, though, is the reason I'm giving him a Fabulous Bartender Award this year. It gives us a glimpse in the soul of a true bartender:

"I remember being behind the bar at **Wild Ginger***, and I was just kind of transitioning by promotion to doing a little bit of bartending. And I remember cleaning up my well, my station, at the end of the night. I was whistling while I worked. And it was so ridiculous. I saw myself above myself – I had this camera on me and I saw myself– and I thought, 'Oh my god, you're happy. Why are you so happy? You're working. What's the matter with you?' That was the turning point. Then from there I started realizing I have to ply my creative intellect while I'm here for these six, seven, eight, nine hours. That's how it really started, and the excitement came, and the passion came, thereafter."* Duggan McDonnell, Cantina, San Francisco. Source: FoodGPS.com by Joshua Lurie.

Jackson Cannon, Boston, MA.

The following, taken from Jackson's bio, will give you some background information on the man:

*"In his twenties Jackson dedicated himself to a career in music, traveling the world in support of such dynamic acts as Eddie Kirkland, Gatemouth Brown, Dennis Brennan and The Tarbox Ramblers. A stint booking music acts at the **Lizard Lounge** in Cambridge, Massachusetts, provided the fortuitous introduction to the craft of bartending and Cannon seized the stage. Settling in Boston, Jackson transitioned out of music and found mixol-*

159

ogy to be the perfect profession for his diverse interests. One part performer, one part philosopher, and a healthy splash of cocktail historian, Cannon has since single-handedly elevated the craft of bartending in Boston.

"Together with three esteemed colleagues, Cannon formed the Jack Rose Society. Dedicated to preserving the legacy of the art of the American cocktail, the Society's mission is to right the wrongs of misunderstood classic cocktails. As opening Bar Manager at **Eastern Standard**, his cocktail program, offering more than 60 classic and new creations, has received national attention. USA Today named Eastern Standard one of the country's Top 10 Hotel Bars, Boston magazine awarded it "Best Restaurant Bar" in 2006, and Esquire magazine included it in its list of "Best Bars in America" in both 2008 and 2010. In 2009, Eastern Standard was awarded top honor of Spirits Hospitality Restaurant of the Year by Santé magazine.

"In 2010, Jackson created the bar program for **Island Creek Oyster Bar**, Eastern Standard's sister restaurant dedicated to bringing the restaurant to the farm by offering guests the opportunity to eat, drink, discover and discuss where our food comes from and learn why it matters. At ICOB, he has uniquely calibrated the contemporary bar program to express the terroir of boutique spirits and highlight seasonality.

"Today, the wanderlust of youth has been channeled into the passion of a true craftsman, leading Jackson to travel in furthering his first-hand knowledge to Turin, Italy, in the study of vermouth; Pisco, Peru, probing the depths of their noble spirit; and Fe Camp, France, in search of the monks of Bénédictine. When he's not traveling or spending time with his wife and two young children, Jackson can be found mentoring the next generation of craft beverage devotees. Of course, there's always a good chance that you'll find him where he's most comfortable, right behind the bar."

Jackson has certainly accomplished much during his career. But here's the quote that got him a Fabulous Bartender Award this year:

"For anyone who wants to tend bar for a living, it's important to remember it's all about service. You won't survive long if that's not in your head and in your heart, but these days, not only do you have all this stuff behind you at the bar, but you have people in front of you, who are willing to have you, the bartender, put it together for them … It's a great time to be mixing drinks." Jackson Cannon, Eastern Standard, Boston. Source: http://www.wbur.org/

Jason Littrell,
New York City, NY.

Jason's a fabulous mixologist, as lots of people already know. He trained under **Sasha Petraske (Milk & Honey, White Star,** and **Little Branch)** at **Randolph at Broom,** and became part of the cocktail dream team at **Death & Co.** To quote from his résumé, Jason has "mixed everything from esoteric drinks to timeless classics and modern innovations, all the while refining his own style and execution."

Jason has also apprenticed at the controlled chaos of Tales of the Cocktail, he sat on three panels at the 2010 Manhattan Cocktail Classic, and he's also done some freelance writing and brand consultation. He was deeply involved in the opening of **Dram**, "a Williamsburg-based cocktail bar where the mixologist plies his craft with a deep appreciation for the special architecture of a great cocktail." And he justly lays claim to having "a natural flair for the kind of breezy service and meticulous execution New Yorkers expect of their bartenders."

I've seen Jason in action and I love his style, but most of all, I love his take on our job. The following quote is the reason I'm hailing Jason Littrell as one of this year's top bartenders:

"Hopefully [the next big trend will be] hospitality. Giving a shit about what you do. Making good drinks is not enough. Being very perceptive of your guests' experience at your bar, THAT is the important thing. And I think that's coming back." Jason Littrell, Dram and Death & Co., New York. Source: wweek.com, October 23, 2010, article by Ruth Brown.

Nicely said, Jason. You're one of this year's best bartenders.

Jessica Gonzalez, New York City, NY.

Jessica has worked at New York joints such as **Death & Co.**, **Five Points Restaurant**, **The Oyster Bar**, **Temple Bar**, **The Old Homestead**, and **The Village Idiot**. You can't get much more well-rounded than that, right? She got the top score in New York at Bar Smarts in 2009, she's an active member of LUPEC (Ladies United for the Preservation of Endangered Cocktails), New York, and she's got lots of other achievements under her belt, too, but none of these things got Jessica a Fabulous Bartender Award this year. I'm handing her the honor just because she knows how to make her guests feel real good when she's behind the bar. I've seen her in action, and I've been impressed by the way she handles herself behind the bar every single time. She knows what the job is all about. Here's what she told me about how she worked her way through the business:

"I have always been in the service industry. I worked for my parents' catering and concession businesses when I was 13. At 16, I was a hostess and went on to be a waitress and bartender at 18. I learned, oddly enough back then in Florida, to work with a jigger and make Manhattans, Rusty Nails, Stingers, and Negronis. I still have a hard time understanding a bartender who works without this basic knowledge. These experiences allowed me to pay my way through school twice, move to NYC, try out several different career paths, travel, and have a heck of a good time at work." It's that last phrase that tells us so damned much about Jessica. She has a heck of a good time at work. You can't do that if you're not a true bartender.

Lynnette Marrero, New York City, NY.

Here's another woman who is full of passion and owns the soul of a true bartender. True, she's not a great croquet player, but not everyone can be good with a mallet, I guess … Let's take a look at Lynette's career. You'll soon understand why she was chosen as one of this year's Fabulous Bartenders. In her own words, then:

*"Lynnette Marrero's 'spirited' career began when she accepted a job at New York's **Flatiron Lounge** alongside cocktail savant **Julie Reiner**. Marrero quickly made the transition from cocktail-waitress to bartender and knew that the spirits industry was her true calling. After learning the ropes at Flatiron Lounge, Marrero became a Senior Bartender at **Freemans NYC** where she devel-*

oped the cocktail menu, ensuring that the restaurant's cuisine was perfectly complemented by her innovative drinks. This led her to consulting and co-designing with Brian Miller the bar program for **Elettaria** in Manhattan's West Village, where she worked closely with the chef to create an award-winning cocktail menu.

"While at Elettaria, Marrero's passion for rum was ignited. Always striving to learn more, Marrero worked to perfect the art of mixing Rums. She spent a week shadowing the Zacapa Rum Master Blender in Guatemala, leading to a year working for Diageo as a Rum Ambassador. Ms. Marrero returned to her career creating bar programs in Manhattan with her company DrinksAt6; cultivating a new generation of cocktail bartenders and elevating the bar at restaurants. As Beverage Director at **Rye House**, Lynnette won Time Out Eat Out Awards for Best New Cocktail Bar, and Best Bar Restaurant Hybrid. She was honored by the James Beard Awards as one of America's Leading Female Mixologists in 2009."

Lynette forgot to mention that she won the prizes for best cocktail in 2009 and in 2010, at Allen Katz' Metropolitan Opera Cocktail Competition. Her drinks are always on the money, but it's her sassiness and her finely-tuned sense of conviviality that earns her a place in this chapter. Who loves you, Lynnette? Besides Ty, I mean… .

Lynn House, Chicago, IL.

I've never met Lynn, but her name has been cropping up in the "best of" cocktail circles for quite a few years now, and her recipes always seem to catch my eye, so I decided to give her a Fabulous Bartender Award simply because she always seems to be pushing the envelope and because more than a couple of people have whispered in my ear about what a caring bartender she is. I'll round this out with a glimpse of some of Lynn's accomplishments, and I think that you'll agree that she deserves mention here:

As of December, 2010, Lynn is Chief Mixologist for the One-Star Michelin-rated restaurant **Blackbird**, in Chicago. Previously she was Chief Mixologist and Beverage Director for **Graham Elliot**, and one of the original Master Bartenders for **The Drawing Room**. Lynn has a BFA in Theatre from Miami University in Oxford, Ohio, she attended the British American Drama Academy in Oxford, England, the Academy of Spirits and Fine Service, and the Advanced Academy of Culinary Mixology (both taught by Bridget Albert). Are you starting to get the picture?

Lynn also passed the Bar Smarts Advanced course, she's a member of the USBG, and she's the Vice President of the Chicago chapter of LUPEC (Ladies United for the Preservation of Endangered Cocktails). She has been highlighted in *The Bartender's Gin Compendium, Cheers, Plate, Night Club and Bar, GQ, Esquire, Ebony, Time Out, Crain's, The Chicago Sun-Times* and *The Chicago Tribune*. And just to round everything out, here's a list of her achievements in the world of cocktail competitions:

2009 National Semi-Finalist Domain de Canton Bartender of the Year

2009 National Finalist Bombay Sapphire/GQ Most Inspired Bartender of the Year

2010 National Finalist Bénédictine/Esquire Alchemist of Our Age

2010 National Finalist 42 Below World Cocktail Cup

2010 Grand Prize Winner Absolut Rebel

2010 National Finalist Shake It Up

2010 National Finalist Bacardi Legacy

Not too shabby, huh? The reason that Lynn is getting this award, though, is that she goes out on a limb when it comes to creating new drinks, and she deserves recognition as a fearless creator. Take a look at the recipe for her drink, Oz, in the 101 Best New Cocktails chapter, and you'll know what I'm talking about. This woman is one of the most courageous bartenders I've never seen. Keep up the good work, Lynn.

Neyah White, San Francisco, CA.

Neyah White, the guy who used to be head bartender at **Nopa** in San Francisco and is now a Brand Ambassador for Suntory, is a good friend of mine, and he's as mindful a bartender as I've ever come across. At Nopa, he taught the staff to think happy thoughts when they pour glasses of water for their guests. "The happiness goes into the water, the water goes into the customer, and soon you have a bar full of happy punters," he said. He also asked his fellow bartenders to hum "New York, New York" when they were making Manhattans, and although he's best known for his creativity in the mixing glass, as far as I'm concerned his strength lies in his commitment to making sure that his guests always have a positive experience when they visit a bar that he's involved with. Neyah is one of my all-time favorite bartenders.

Salvatore Calabrese, London, UK.

PART 4 • OTHER PEOPLE'S STUFF

I wrote the following piece for Drinkology.com, the Pernod-Ricard bartender community web site. It will help you understand why Salvatore Calabrese deserves this award.

I think that I first visited **Salvatore at FIFTY** *in 2006, and as a lad who was dragged up in a pub on a council estate in Lancashire (which, BTW, ended up being one of the best things that ever happened to me), I must say that I was secretly thinking, "Oh, if only Mum and Dad could see me now." It's hard not to let your ego have a bit of fun now and again, though I try to keep him under control as much as possible. And speaking of egos … Salvatore was, and as many of you will know is, the consummate host. He's sophisticated, smart, dapper, has an accent that makes me feel vaguely gay for the man, and yes, as we all know, Salvatore has this, how can I put it … hmm … perhaps GIGANTIC EGO fits the bill. It's true, Salvatore does have a big ego, but in my opinion, his ego is nothing more than a façade. I've seen the other side of this man, you see. And the other side is, I think, the side that puts S@50 solidly into my list of all-time fave bars.*

About ten minutes after I first set foot into Salvatore's bar, the bartenders started to take the piss out of me. I was pretty flabbergasted. And I was in heaven. I love it when bartenders take the piss out of me, but I never expected it to happen at the oh-so-posh club where The Maestro himself reigned. I was expecting "yes sir, no sir, three bags full, sir," and although I hate that kind of thing, that is what I was expecting that night.

I know I'm going to screw up the facts here, because I was two-sheets-to-the wind when Salvatore told me the story, but I think I remember the basic underlying message in this tale. And this, in my opinion, is what makes Salvatore a true maestro.

At one of Salvatore's very first jobs, when he was but a lad, every day he had to take a drink down to the chef in the kitchens. It happened at the same time every day, and every day Salvatore would walk into the kitchen with a smile on his face and present the chef with his drink along with a few friendly words. One day, for no apparent reason, the chef took that drink, hurled it across the kitchen, and screamed at Salvatore to get out of his sight. Salvatore ran, but later, he went back to ask the chef why he'd done what he'd done.

"I was in a bad mood," said the chef. "And if you want to be a bartender you must learn how to read people before you start your encounter with them. If you had intuited my mood, you'd have been quieter, you wouldn't have smiled so much, and you might have just put my drink down and left me to stew in my own juices. Until you learn to do that, you'll never be a good bartender."

Salvatore certainly learned that lesson well, and I believe that he taught it to his staff at S@50, too. That's why they started taking the piss out of me right after I first set foot in the place. The ascertained my personality, and they ran with it. They truly cared about making me happy.

Stan Vadrna, Bratislava, Slovakia.

It's hard for me to know where to start when I try to explain just how important Stan Vadrna has been in my life. He's one of the most accomplished bartenders I know, the level of his passion for the craft is off the charts, and like the Energizer Bunny, he just keeps going, and going, and going. And although Stan might be a master of the hard shake and an expert in many different aspects of our craft, the true beauty of his philosophy lies in his mantra: *Ichigo ichie*, the Japanese phrase meaning, loosely, "One encounter, one opportunity." The following text first appeared in my *Path of the Bartender* column in *The Bartender Bulletin*. It will serve to show you why Stan got a Fabulous Bartender Award this year.

When Stan Vadrna applied to come to one of my Cocktails in the Country workshops in 2005—that's the year that my jumbled records indicate—he told me that the reason he wanted to join the class was because, and I quote, "Knowledge is God." And Stan Vadrna is certainly a guy with a huge thirst for knowledge.

I found it hard to believe that someone would travel from Slovakia to come to one of my classes, so when he first applied I insisted that he send me a $100 deposit to secure a space. "That's the last I'll hear from this guy," I thought. Three days later I received an email from Stan telling me to pick up the C-note at a specific branch of Western Union located in a supermarket no more than 10 minutes from my house. The man was serious.

Since that time, Stan and I have become close friends. He has trained in Japan, tended bar in Manhattan, and he's gone on to international acclaim as one of the world's very best bartenders, and along the way our paths have crossed time and time again, **173** often at trade events, but also at the Slovakia Bar Awards in 2007, when Stan helped me get a gig as a judge, alongside the **Wonderful Angus Winchester**, and in 2008 I was very proud to be co-best man, with the fat-washing **Eben Freeman**, at Stan's wedding to Yasmin. We're good buddies, Stan and I. Soul mates, I think.

We had a little free time in Bratislava during the Slovakia event, so Stan and I sought and found a great tattoo artist and invested in a little of his handiwork. I had an image of a sun, surrounding a yin-yang symbol that could be mistaken for sea waves—all my tats are connected to water—and Stan got his Japanese mantra, ichigo ichie (ITCH-igo ITCH-ee-ay), engraved on his forearm.

Ichigo ichie is a Japanese phrase that's connected to both Zen Buddhism and to the Japanese Tea Ceremony. It can be translated in a number of ways, since subtleties can be lost in translation, but to Stan Vadrna, it means "one encounter, one opportunity." He takes it with him whenever he's behind the bar, so when a customer is lucky enough to walk into a bar where Stan Vadrna is holding court, s/he will always be treated to the most attentive service. Stan knows that he has but one chance to impress his guests, and he takes advantage of this opportunity by always being the best he can be. Stan Vadrna is a bartender in every sense of the word. Stan Vadrna walks the path.

If all of us bear this in mind when we're behind the stick, we can make this world of ours a far better place. One encounter at a time.

… Lest you think that Stan Vadrna is one helluva serious dude, I should tell you about the time when he and I were behind the bar together at Painter's, my local joint in Cornwall-on-Hudson. He was preparing drinks for two people at the end of the bar who had just bumped into each other. "What are you making, Stan?" I asked.

"Ah, the man. The man just have dinner, so for him I make nice digestivo cocktail. He will like this," Stan told me in his thick Slovak accent as he stirred his creation.

"And for the woman?" I enquired.

"For the woman," said Stan, "I make drink that's full of sexual tension."

Ichigo ichie, *Stan,* ichigo ichie.

SARGASSO SEAS OF INFELICITY

"Maidens wed without champagne … are destined to become husband beaters. Ships launched without the surge of amber bubbles on their prows are doomed to drift in Sargasso seas of infelicity."

Crosby Gaige's Cocktail Guide and Ladies Companion by Crosby Gaige, 1945.

Chapter 2

Fabulous Innovators

The number of innovative new techniques that has been incorporated into our craft over the past five years or so is really spectacular, and I think that it's important to start to document who has brought what to the party so that we can give the innovators their due respect, encourage others to push the envelope even further, and let future generations know exactly what went down during the cocktail revolution that we've all played a part in during the first decade of the twenty-first century.

There will, I'm pretty sure, be repercussions from this chapter. There will be bartenders who think that they introduced this or invented that, and did it long before the people who I'm highlighting in this chapter. And they might be right. I promise, though, that at the time of writing I, and every person I'm about to detail here, believe that the details I'm about to lay down here are true.

I should also note that more people deserve mention in this category than I've managed to include, but time and space prevent me from detailing every single innovator here. I'll play catch-up in future editions of the *Annual Manual*, and meanwhile, please feel free to get in touch with me at gary@ar-dentspirits.com if you feel as though you, or a friend of yours, deserves mention in this category.

These Fabulous Innovators are listed in alpha-order by first name. These are some of the people who I think deserve to be noted for posterity, and given the respect that they deserve by us, their peers behind the bar.

Eben Freeman, New York City, NY.

Innovation: Fat-Washing.

I'm real happy to be able to tell my brother and sister bartenders all over the world the true story behind who developed the fat-washing technique of infusing fat-laden ingredients (such as bacon) into a distilled spirit (such as bourbon). Eben Freeman does not, and has never, claimed to have been the first to pioneer this technique, but I'm hailing him as the innovator of this technique, because I believe he's the guy who took the method and ran with it, bringing it into (almost) mainstream methodology.

Eben told me that the idea for fat-washing came to him from Chef **Sam Mason**, when they were both working at **WD-50**, the Manhattan restaurant that was a "shrine to molecular gastronomy," and in turn, it seems, Mason had gotten the idea from perfumers who use fat-washing to extract aromas from substances that they couldn't retrieve by maceration.

And now the tale of fat-washing gets even more intriguing: In the world of drinks, it's been going on for centuries. That's right. Centuries.

My old friend **David Wondrich**, the cheapest man on the face of the earth, the guy who hasn't had his hand in his pocket for so long that they are probably filled with pieces of eight, the man who claims that I'm a rogue and a scoundrel—okay, I'll cop to that—is the guy who found a recipe that involves fat-washing that dates back a few hundred years. In his book,

180

Punch: *The Delights (and Dangers) of The Flowing Bowl,* Dave points to Milk Punch, variations of which have been around since the 1600s, as a drink that called for fat-washing, and in my estimation the bastard's right. Guess I'd better buy him yet another drink.

The Milk Punch that Dave describes contains citrus juice that curdles the milk when it's added to the bowl. The curds are then strained from the punch, rendering a drink that is "exceptionally smooth and creamy-tasting without actually being creamy." Nicely found, Dave, and nicely recognized, too.

Back to Eben Freeman: I spent about a week in France with Eben and other bar types such as **Jim Meehan** a few years back on a press trip where we were run ragged by marketer Jean-Louis Carbonnier, who organized this grueling adventure. I'm here to tell you that Eben is the real deal: He's a true innovator and he has the soul of a bartender. I'm proud to call you a friend, Eben. And remember, it's all about the terroir.

Here are some recipes from Eben. I've edited them slightly, but for the most part I've let him tell it in his own tongue.

Brown Butter Rum

Put 1 lb of sweet butter in a large saucepan, heat until solids in butter separate and turn dark brown (stirring often), then pour one liter of Flor de Cana 7 year rum in hot butter, being extremely careful not to spill rum over open flame and keeping one's head out of the way of the resulting steam. [Hint from gaz: take the saucepan off the stove and away from the flame while you do this.] Stir rum and butter mixture together, allow it to come to room temperature, and transfer to a large container.

Place the container in the refrigerator and let it sit 48 hours. Use a spoon to remove the fat on top of the mixture, then strain the rum through a fine-mesh strainer, then a coffee filter, to remove solids. [Hint from gaz: you could use a double layer of dampened cheesecloth in a strainer to remove all solids in one fell swoop.]

The Crumble

60 ml (2 oz) Brown Butter Rum

15 ml (.5 oz) Philip's of Bristol Pink Clove Cordial

30 to 60 ml (1 to 2 oz) Eric Bordelet's Poire Granit wine

Freshly ground nutmeg, as an aromatic garnish

Shake the rum and the cordial over ice and strain into an old-fashioned glass containing one large ice cube. Add the Poire Granit wine, dust with freshly ground nutmeg.

Francesco Turrini, London, UK & Christina Bini, New York City, NY.

Innovation: Martini Stones.

Martini Stones—porous pebbles infused with liquid ingredients and added to cocktails and mixed drinks—are not a new innovation. Francesco Turrini told me he got the idea from Stephen Visakay's *Vintage Bar Ware*, 1997, wherein he read about people adding vermouth-soaked stones to chilled gin in order to make ultra-dry Martinis. And in *Martini Straight Up: The Classic American Cocktail*, Lowell Edmunds, cites a certain Fred Pool as being the inventor of marble Martini Stones, which Pool credited for making the vermouth taste better by neutralizing the acid therein. Sounds like hooey to me, but...

I found out about Francesco's method—soaking pebbles in sherry with a couple of other ingredients, storing them in the freezer, and adding two or three stones to a glass of Zacapa 23-year-old rum—when he sent me the recipe for his new drink, On the Rocks. You can find it in the 101 Best New Cocktails chapter. Then I read an article in *The New York Times* about **Christina Bini** using vermouth-soaked stones in her Dry Gin Martinis at **Il Matto**, Matteo Boglione's restaurant in TriBeCa. Robert Simonson wrote that piece, so I dashed off a few questions to him. Here's what he had to say:

183

Q: Could you tell me a little about Christina Bini, the Italian bartender at Il Matto, Matteo Boglione's TriBeCa restaurant?

A: Bini is a mixologist from Florence. She made a big splash there at a restaurant called Fusion, creating drinks from unusual vegetal and savory ingredients such as lettuce, balsamic vinegar, peperoncini, Parmigiamo cheese, beet juice, tomatoes and zucchini. The owners of Il Matto convinced her to come to New York and run the drinks program at Il Matto.

Q: I'm especially interested in her use of vermouth-soaked stones in her Martinis, could you tell me about this, please?

A: Bini's debut menu at Il Matto offered two Martinis, both featuring as their garnish stones soaked in vermouth. One had a black stone from Mongolia, the other a white stone from the Liguria region in northwest Italy. How they got these stones, I have no idea. The rocks were soaked in vermouth for at least 12 hours before being placed in the drinks. Bini said she came up with the idea herself, but the notion has some history. Lowell Edmunds, in his 2003 book Martini, Straight Up, *tells of one Fred Pool who became known for soaking stones in vermouth in the late 1960s, when people preferred super-dry Martinis. So the idea is not exactly new. Still, it's a novel, and frankly eccentric, approach.*

Q: Did you taste one of these Martinis?

A: Yes. I sampled both sorts of Martinis.

Q: Was the vermouth discernible?

A: I have to say yes, you could taste the vermouth. More importantly, the influence of the vermouth was different in each drink, showing that the rock thing wasn't completely a gimmick. The white Ligurian stones were more porous, and came from a place nearer to the sea. Therefore, they soaked up, and then released, more vermouth into the drink. They also lent the drink a salty, mineral aspect. I much preferred the Martini with the white stone. The one with the smooth black stones tasted very much like large glasses of gin.

I don't doubt for a second that Christina came up with this idea without any knowledge of this method being used in the sixties, ands she took it a step further, I think, by selecting different stones to create different styles of Martinis. Francesco, on the other hand, will readily tell everyone that he learned the technique from research, but he's put this methodology to really good use, and he deserves much credit here as one of this year's most innovative bartenders.

Jamie Boudreau, Seattle, WA.

Innovations: Mist-Flaming, Herb-Spanking, Egg-Frothing, and various other Scintillating Skills.

I used to really like this guy until he told me that his Dad is the same age as I am, so now I pretty much hate him, but I can't deny that he has brought lots and lots of innovations to our craft. And he's done it without ever taking himself too seriously, and without ever taking his eye off the ball, and with understanding that service is what our job is all about. Congrats, Jamie. It's almost as if you know what you're doing.... .

Although Jamie is known to lots of people for his skills in molecular mixology, that's not the part of the craft that he himself sees as his forte. He's proud of his palate, though, and there are some techniques that he thinks he's probably responsible for bringing to the craft.

Jamie was the first bartender to put bitters and/or spirits into an atomizer, then spray them onto a drink through a flame so that they ignite as they travel to their destination. It's not only effective, it's downright showy. I like that. Jamie also thinks that he was probably the first bartender to spank herbs rather than muddle them, thus releasing their flavors and aromas without punishing them too much or releasing the bitter elements from the stalks.

And one more thing that Jamie Boudreau brought to the forefront of twenty-first-century bartending techniques is the use of an electric, or battery-operated, milk frother for emulsifying eggs in a cocktail (he also uses a copper shaker for drinks that call for raw eggs).

Jamie Boudreau Quotation: "Gary Regan taught me that you can be an ass and still succeed in this business."

Learn from Jamie: I was going to detail some of Jamie's methodology in this book, but the book decided that it would rather use the space to shout out more bartenders, so instead, I'm going to suggest that you go learn at the feet of the Cocktail Whisperer himself by visiting http://spiritsandcocktails. wordpress.com, and/or http://www.smallscreennetwork. com/raising_the_bar/

Ross Simon,
Arizona U.S.B.G.
by way of the Lab Bar,
London, UK.

Innovation: Carbonated Cocktails.

Ross currently works for Southern Wine & Spirits, and he helped form the Arizona Chapter of the U.S.B.G., but he started out in the bar biz by working at his family's restaurant in Scotland, then moved to London where he eventually became the head bartender at the famed **Lab Bar**. He moved to Arizona in 2006.

Ross came to my attention when he submitted a recipe for consideration in this book—see Kaffir Lime Gimlet—and in the methodology he instructed to "use one of the new soda stream machines" to carbonate the drink. I wasn't sure if he was being serious so I emailed him to ask about this and here's his response: "Serious as heart attack my friend, I'm just the first (maybe craziest) … **Colin Appiah** was in town and I made him one and he was blown away."

Well, as far as I know Ross Simon *was* the first to use a Soda-Stream machine to carbonate cocktails. I bought one two days later and I've been playing with it ever since. If you try this, know that some cocktails tend to hold the carbonation better than others, and as a rule of thumb, you'll probably find that drinks such as Daiquirís, which call for citrus juice, tend to get fizzier than, say, Manhattans. God only knows why you'd want a fizzy Manhattan, though… .

Ryan C. Maybee, Kansas City, MO.

Innovation: Smoked Whiskey.

"I wanted to submit a couple recipes for your new book. In the newsletter you mention new innovative techniques, and I believe this qualifies. I've included a link to a YouTube video demonstrating the process of smoking the whiskey and the making of the cocktail," wrote Ryan C. Maybee, owner of **Manifesto** in Kansas City, MO, when he sent me the recipe for Smokin' Choke (recipe below).

Ryan uses a Polyscience Smoking Gun, a hand-held device usually used for smoking small quantities of food, to smoke bourbon for his drink. He attaches a hose to the device, puts the hose into the bourbon in a large container, leaving air-room at the top of the vessel. Next he burns applewood and peachwood in his smoking gun, and the smoke travels through a hose that's placed into the vessel that's filled with bourbon. He allows smoke to fill the air space atop the whiskey, then he lowers the hose into the liquid and it bubbles through the whiskey itself. It takes just a few minutes.

You can see Ryan smoking the bourbon at this url: http://www.youtube.com/watch?v=7wQ5JhbsF-g

And you can see him make the drink here: http://www.youtube.com/watch?v=hWxqv9pbUoc&feature=related

I asked Ryan how he'd come up with this concept. Here's what he had to say: "The idea came from a couple different sources, one being I believe **Eben Freeman**. If I remember correctly, he was smoking Coca-Cola for a drink he called The Waylon. I was pretty fascinated by the concept, but everything I found online involved a long process of smoking in an actual smoker. When I found the Polyscience Smoking Gun, I just thought I'd give it a shot and see what happens. It worked out really well, the smoke aroma and flavor were pronounced, and after multiple experiments I also found that by smoking a bottle for just five minutes the infusion takes and doesn't dissipate over time. As for the Smokin' Choke Cocktail, I was influenced by **Don Lee** and his Benton's Old-Fashioned. The use of maple syrup made great sense, and just taking a simple, classic approach with a drink like a sling or Old-Fashioned would be the best way to showcase and balance the smoky flavors. The straightforward Old-Fashioned was just too sweet, so I added the uber-bitter Cynar to temper the sweetness.

"The smoke infusion is really interesting. Tasting it neat, you definitely get the smoky aromatics and applewood flavors, but once you add even a drop of water or a cube of ice the smoke just pops out of it. I've tried using it in shaken cocktails with citrus, like a sour or a Ward Eight, and it just doesn't work, the smoke dominates everything. I think the use of powerful ingredients like the grade B maple, Peychaud's, and Cynar is the best way to balance it."

Smokin' Choke

60 ml (2 oz) applewood-smoked Four Roses bourbon

1 barspoon Cynar

15 ml (.5 oz) grade B maple syrup

4 dashes Peychaud's bitters

1 orange twist, as garnish

PART 4 • OTHER PEOPLE'S STUFF

Stir over ice and strain into chilled old-fashioned glassed
with one large cube. Add the garnish.

gaz sez: *I didn't test this one, simply cos I'm too cheap to lay out the bread for the equipment, but I did ask Ryan for a testimonial, and here's what came back at me:*

"Ryan Maybee of Manifesto asked if I would give you a testimonial for the Smokin' Choke Cocktail that they prepare at his incredible bar. I am a huge fan of this cocktail but think they need to rename it. Sure the Smokin' Choke is very clever and explanatory of the cocktail but I just call it the Tastiest Cocktail in America! The layers of flavor in this cocktail are truly amazing and it is in my opinion flawless. The way the orange and the artichoke play off of each other with the underlying light not overpowering smoke flavor from the bourbon carries through your palate is simply amazing."—**John McClure**, Chef/Owner, **Starker's Restaurant**, 201 W. 47th St., Kansas City, MO.

Tony Conigliaro, London, UK & Jeffrey Morgenthaller, Portland, OR.

Innovation: Aging Cocktails.

As far as I know, **Tony Conigliaro**, London's much-loved crazy-bastard bartender who owns **69 Colebrooke Row** (69ColebrookeRow.com), a fabulous joint that I frequent as often as is humanly possible, was the first to start bottle-aging his cocktails, and after sampling one of his aged Manhattans, I can attest that this process is well worth a try.

> **gaz sez:** *Aging in glass is a subtle way of oxidizing, thus evolving, cocktails, and when I experimented with this I employed a trick taught to me by an artisanal eau-de-vie distiller in Italy some years ago. Every four weeks I transfer the aging cocktails from one bottle to another. This gives the drink a chance to aerate a little, and it oxidizes a bit faster, too. Cocktails aged using this methodology are usually ready to serve after a few months, and they get to be pretty extraordinary if left for a year or more.*

You can try aging cocktails in wood, too, and you'll notice changes in these drinks occur far faster than the bottle-aged cocktails. **Jeffrey Morgenthaler**, head bartender at **Clyde**

193

Common in Portland, Oregon, did just this after being inspired by Tony C's aged cocktails during a visit to London.

Morgenthaler has aged rye-based Manhattans in a small, used Madeira cask, and that batch was declared perfect after five to six weeks. Then he bought used whiskey casks (http://stores.intuitwebsites.com/TuthilltownSpirits) and filled them with Negronis. "After six weeks in the bourbon barrel, our Negroni emerged a rare beauty. The sweet vermouth so slightly oxidized, the color paler and rosier than the original, the mid-palate softly mingled with whiskey, the finish long and lingering with oak tannins," he wrote in his blog (www.jeffreymorgenthaler.com).

Here are a couple of Jeffrey's recipes to get your juices flowing.

Aged Negroni

Makes approximately 11.25 liters, or around 3 gallons

Adapted from a recipe by Jeffrey Morgenthaler, Clyde Common, Portland, OR.

5 750-ml bottles dry gin
5 750-ml bottles sweet vermouth
5 750-ml bottles Campari

Stir ingredients together without ice and pour into a 3-gallon oak barrel. Allow to rest for 5 to 7 weeks, then pour into glass bottles, filtering out any particles of wood or other unwanted debris from the barrel. Stir individual drinks–approximately 90 ml (3 oz)–over ice, and strain into a chilled cocktail glass.

Aged Manhattan

Makes approximately 11.25 liters, or around 3 gallons

Adapted from a recipe by Jeffrey Morgenthaler, Clyde Common, Portland, OR.

10 750-ml bottles straight rye whiskey

5 750-ml bottles sweet vermouth

210 ml (7 oz) Angostura bitters

Stir ingredients together without ice and pour into a 3-gallon oak barrel (Morgenthaler prefers barrels that have previously stored sherry, Madeira, or port wine). Allow to rest for 5 to 7 weeks, then pour into glass bottles, filtering out any particles of wood or other unwanted debris from the barrel. Stir individual drinks–approximately 90 ml (3 oz)–over ice, and strain into a chilled cocktail glass.

A BAD GAMBLING HABIT,
A PENSION FOR LOOSE WOMEN
AND FAST CARS

What made you get into bartending? "Easy money. People with a certain personality are naturally drawn to places where you can be on stage. Wait, are you actually quoting me? Let's say something fun. A bad gambling habit, a pension for loose women and fast cars."

Viken Koundakjian at Westport Lounge, DesMoines, IA.
Source: http://www.desmoinesregister.com/, 2010.

The 101 Best New Cocktails

Almost 2,000 recipes were sent to me for consideration for this list, I eyeballed them down to 211, tested those recipes (many, many thanks go to Sal and Pete at Painter's, Cornwall-on-Hudson, New York, for letting me use the Gallery bar and lots of their stock), and whittled the list down to the 101 recipes in this chapter. Phew. That was hard work.

I confess to included a few, not many but a few, drinks that were created by people who don't actually work behind the bar. I was very choosy, though. Honest. And most of them used to be bartenders and have now gone on to lesser pursuits such as, say, being a brand ambassador or something.... And finally I need to mention that, to the best of my knowledge, the bars and cities mentioned in each recipe were the bars and cities where the bartender who created the drink worked when they submitted the recipe. Some have switched bars, some have switched cities, and at least one guy switched continents. It's really tough to keep up with yous guys.

I saw lots of innovation this year, and thankfully we also saw a big swing back toward simplicity, too. Not too simple, mind, but instead of going overboard with root-beer reductions and the like, I noticed ingredients such as dry vermouth infused with flavored tea, and smoky scotches being used in tiny quantities to add tons of complexity to the glass without the pretensions of some of the more overboard ingredients I'd been witnessing in, say, 2008 and 2009.

This isn't to say that some bartenders out there aren't still intent on pushing the envelope, but it's starting to look as though that job is being left to them as can do it well. Thank God for that, huh?

Genever is still on the rise, it seems, and if genever producers don't buy **Dave Wondrich** a mansion or a Lear Jet or something for leading the charge on this front, they'll be doing him a disservice. And I've also noticed more and more fortified wines—mainly sherry and port—being called for in new cocktails. They make for good bases and can also serve well as modifiers, too.

I'm surprised to see that pisco hasn't yet gained a strong foothold behind cocktailian bars, so I'm mentioning that here in the hope that more bartenders will start tinkering with it in the near future. Pisco can serve the shaker very well indeed.

I didn't include the following drink as one of the top 101 cocktails, but I thought that I'd start a convention of bringing you the recipe that I'm most proud of creating each year. I featured this drink in *The San Francisco Chronicle*, and the text that follows will clue you in on the drink's origins. Hope you enjoy it.

A Very Cooperative Cocktail

I was asked recently to create a drink for a food cooperative that was holding an event to raise some money so they could keep on promoting sustainable thises and organic thats, and since I'm a sucker for this sort of thing, and the co-op was founded by friends of mine to boot, I told them I'd give it a shot.

When this sort of challenge comes along, providing I have the time, I like to mull on ingredients for a few days, sorting them out in my head and seeing if I can put them together intuitively before I actually mix them up in a shaker. For some reason cherry brandy came to mind in this case, and I figured I'd throw some cognac into the mix, too, along with a few dashes of Angostura, and perhaps a little brewed tea. I've never really played with tea in a cocktail, and I thought that, if I was going to keep up with my younger bartender friends, I should probably give it a go.

A few days went by, and on a balmy afternoon, when I tired of sitting on the deck watching the squirrels sliding down the recently Crisco'd pole that holds the bird-feeders, I headed for the kitchen to put the drink together. I saw at once that cognac wasn't going to be the base at all—I had only one bottle, and it was a very expensive bottle, at that. No way the co-op was getting their hands on it.

And my karma caught up with me on the Angostura front, too. There was barely enough bitters in the bottle to get me through one or two Manhattans, and it was getting close to five of the clock. I'd have to rethink this thing.

I had quite a stock of aged rum on hand, so that became the base of the drink, but what would I do about the lack of bitters? As I rifled through the pantry, searching for teas to use in the drink, karma changed her mind about me when she offered up a box of chai tea bags that had been sitting there for a month or three. Chai is spicy, I thought, and it's complex, too. It had to be worth a try, right?

I brewed the chai using half as much water as normal, then I added ice cubes that melted pretty quickly giving me a cool brew that was just about the right strength—it's a good little trick to stash under your belt.

Next I was faced with deciding on what sort of ratios I going to use. Since this wasn't a case of pimping a classic drink, I had no template to work from, and since I'd never used chai in a drink before, I had no experience with the stuff as a cocktail ingredient. I figured that I'd make the drink using equal amounts of rum, cherry brandy, and chai, and I'd add a little simple syrup for good measure. Once I tasted that, I figured, I'd have a decent idea on where to go from there. Guess what? I nailed this drink in one fell swoop. It's a very cooperative cocktail.

A Very Cooperative Cocktail

Recipe by gaz regan. Created for the Cornwall Community Co-Op, Cornwall-on-Hudson, New York, for a benefit featuring John Charles Thomas on trumpet and Bari Mort at the piano, July, 2010.

30 ml (1 oz) aged rum

30 ml (1 oz) Cherry Heering*

30 ml (1 oz) cold brewed chai tea

15 ml (.5 oz) simple syrup (1:1)

1 lemon twist, as garnish

Stir over ice and strain into a chilled champagne coupe. Add the garnish.

*I actually used a Sour Cherry Cordial that's made that's close to where I live in the Hudson Valley at the Warwick Valley Winery & Distillery. I highly recommend their products. Find them at http://wvwinery.com/.

IT'S NOT ABOUT ME

Q: What's the biggest lesson you've learned behind the bar?

A: It's not about me. It's about the guest. You can get a bit arrogant because we've got a great cocktail program, and you're part of that. But the guest's experience is the real measure of your work."

Jason Asher, who runs the Jade Bar at Sanctuary Camelback Mountain Resort & Spa, Arizona.

Source: *The Arizona Republic*, November 20, 2010.

The 101 Best
New Cocktails

After-Dinner Sazerac

Adapted from a recipe by
**Giancarlo Quiroz Jesus,
Corner Bar**, Auckland, New Zealand.

"This cocktail was a semi-finalist for the New Zealand
Suntory Cup Cocktail Competition 2010, chosen out of
100. Easy to drink and make, definitely the cocktail after a
well deserved dinner."
—Giancarlo Quiroz Jesus.

Galliano Ristretto, as rinse

1 dash Angostura bitters

1 sugar cube

60ml (2 oz) Yamazaki Single Malt 12-Year-Old whisky

1 kaffir lime leaf

Rinse a chilled old-fashioned glass with the Ristretto,
then discard excess. Combine bitters and sugar cube
in a mixing glass and dissolve, then add whisky and ice.
Stir and strain into the prepared glass. Break or "crack"
the leaf in four different places lengthwise over the drink
to get the aromas out, then run it over the rim of the
glass and discard.

gaz sez: *Wow, this is a cracking drink. It's great
to see the Galliano Ristretto put to good use in this
one, and I love that Giancarlo chose to work with
the Yamazaki 12-Year-Old—it's a great bottling.
The lime leaf garnish does add a special little something to this drink, but if you've none on hand, the
cocktail works very well without it.*

All Betts Are Off

Adapted from a recipe by
**Matt Lanning,
The Bitter Bar**, Boulder, CO.

"Not many of my current customers can find a way to enjoy the smokiness of mezcal. In looking for a drink to help
them understand the versatility of the spirit, I wanted to
come up with something spiritous but that retained the
character of the mezcal. The drink has been well received by
all but the most smoke-sensitive.... The name is in hom-
age to Sombra's owner, Richard Betts, and refers to the way
that the cocktail might just change a non-believer's opinion
about mezcal. You think you don't like mezcal? With this
one, all 'betts' are off!"
—Matt Lanning.

45 ml (1.5 oz) Sombra mezcal

22.5 ml (.75 oz) Dolin Blanc vermouth

22.5 ml (.75 oz) yellow Chartreuse

2 dashes grapefruit bitters (I use Bitter Truth)

1 grapefruit twist, as garnish

Stir over ice and strain into a chilled cocktail glass.
Squeeze the twist over the drink, then add as garnish.

gaz sez: *When I eyeballed this recipe the Dolin
didn't make much sense to me, but when I tasted
the drink it was obvious why Matt had chosen this
particular vermouth to ride alongside mezcal and
Chartreuse—two very dominant ingredients. The
Dolin brings a creaminess to this quaff, it turns
out—it acts like a white fluffy mattress on which
the other ingredients play.*

Andean Dusk

Adapted from a recipe by
**Meaghan Dorman,
Raines Law Room**, New York City, NY.

4 red grapes

15 ml (.5 oz) fresh lemon juice

15 ml (.5 oz) simple syrup

30 ml (1 oz) La Diablada pisco

90 ml (3 oz) rosé champagne

Muddle the grapes in a mixing glass. Add ice and the
remaining ingredients except champagne. Shake
and strain into a chilled champagne flute. Top with
champagne.

gaz sez: *Pisco! I'm editing these recipes out of alpha-order and I've worked on over 70 of the 101
cocktails on this list before I came upon this, the
first pisco-based drink I've seen thus far. Thanks,
Meaghan! Nice and simple and well thought out,
too.*

Another Fine Mes

Adapted from a recipe by
Brendan F. Casey,
Café Centro, New York City, NY.

"I'm always trying to come up with new variations of the Manhattan (Dale DeGroff's Man O' War recipe changed my life), and I loves me some tequila! My Lady and I just picked up some maple syrup at the local greenmarket one day, and I wanted to use it in a cocktail, so there you have it. Cheers!"
—Brendan Casey.

1/2 teaspoon maple syrup (fresh local!)

60 ml (2 oz) Michter's straight rye whiskey

30 ml (1 oz) Don Julio reposado tequila

15 ml (.5 oz) Combier liqueur d'orange

15 ml (.5 oz) Punt e Mes

2 dashes Fee Brothers Old Fashion bitters

2 dashes Regans' Orange Bitters No. 6

1 orange twist, as garnish

Stir the syrup, rye, and tequila in a mixing glass. Add ice and the remaining ingredients. Stir while thinking about Laurel and Hardy. Strain into a chilled cocktail glass. Add the garnish.

gaz sez: *First I should note that Dale's Man O' War, made with 45 ml (1.5 oz) Wild Turkey 101, 30 ml (1 oz) orange curaçao, and 15 ml (.5 oz) each of sweet vermouth and fresh lemon juice, shaken with (optional) slices of orange and lemon in the shaker and garnished with an orange slice*

209

*and a cherry, is a fabulous drink, and it shows off
Dale's ability to put a simple drink together wherein the finished product is far, far greater than the
sum of its ingredients.*

Brendan F. Casey's Another Fine Mes cocktail, though, is a drink of another color. I'm not a big fan of maple syrup in cocktails, but in this drink it plays with the Punt e Mes beautifully—a combination I'd never have dreamed of. Then take a look at the base spirits: Michter's rye and Don Julio tequila? Great products both, but Casey must be out of his head, I thought, to put both of them in the same shaker. Wrong again, gaz. I have no idea why this combination works so well, but there's a complexity in this drink that lifts the soul to new heights.

I tried the Another Fine Mes using Cointreau instead of the Combier, and it still worked well. Substituting Grand Marnier works, too, though it renders a cocktail that's a little sweeter than the original. Nice work, Brendan.

Atom Limo

Adapted from a recipe by
**Stephan Hinz,
Shepheard American Bar**, Cologne, Germany.

"Cheers!"
—Stephan Hinz.

35 ml (1.17 oz) Wild Turkey bourbon

35 ml (1.17 oz) Lustau Pedro Ximenez sherry

15 ml (.5 oz) fresh lemon juice

40 ml (1.33 oz) fresh apple juice

2 pieces ginger

Ginger ale

1 mint sprig, as garnish

1 apple slice, as garnish

1 fresh cherry, as garnish

Build in a marmalade glass over ice. Add the garnishes.

gaz sez: *I met Stephan in France during the G'Vine Gin Bartender Competition in 2010, and I've got to say that he is one intense bartender! Nice guy, too. I love that he kept this drink simple. It's something that can be made at most decent cocktail bars, and it delivers a really nice punch, too.*

Autumn Breeze

Adapted from a recipe by
**Jo-Jo Valenzuela,
Ris**, Washington, D.C.

"I wanted to create a simple cocktail that has fall written all over it. Denise, a regular of mine, was the first to try the drink and named it Autumn Breeze. Minutes later her boyfriend Alan arrived, tried the drink, and claimed that it is the best cocktail he has ever had in his life. That was a nice moment, here's to them!"
—Jo-Jo Valenzuela.

45 ml (1.5 oz) Laird's applejack

60 ml (2 oz) cranberry juice

Juice of lemon wedge

1 splash simple syrup

3 dashes Peychaud's bitters

1 lemon twist, as garnish

1 apple slice, as garnish

Build in a rocks glass full of ice. Roll. Add the garnishes (release a mist of lemon twist over the drink to work wonders on its aroma).

gaz sez: *Peychaud's, Peychaud's, Peychaud's! Here's yet another example of a really simple formula that springs off the high-board and does a double somersault on its way down the throat. And it's all down to the Peychaud's in this case. Who'd have thunk it? Well, Jo-Jo Valenzuela, I guess. Denise and Alan are lucky to have Jo-Jo as their bartender, huh?*

213

Baldwin Apple

Adapted from a recipe by
Ran Duan,
Sichuan Garden 2, Boston, MA.

"This cocktail is named after the building that my restaurant is in, The Baldwin Mansion. It was built in 1661 and from what I've read, the Baldwin apple was first seeded on the family's farm."
—Ran Duan.

45 ml (1.5 oz) calvados

30 ml (1 oz) fresh lemon juice

30 ml (1 oz) Spice Syrup*

15 ml (.5 oz) Fee Brothers falernum

15 ml (.5 oz) Fee Brothers orgeat

1 egg white

Grated nutmeg, as garnish

Dry-shake, then add ice. Hard-shake and strain into a chilled coupe. Add the garnish.

*Spice Syrup: Combine 2 cinnamon sticks, 2 star anise, 9 cloves, 4 cardamom pods, and about 2L (8 cups) water in a large saucepan. Bring to boil, reduce the heat, and simmer for 15 minutes until you get a nice light golden color from spice. Then add 1,200 g (6 cups) sugar and stir and simmer for 5 more minutes. Cool and transfer to bottles. This should make enough for about two 750-ml bottles.

gaz sez: *The spice syrup used in the Baldwin Apple is a great ingredient to have on hand during the cold-weather months. I used it to make Hot Toddies, and I added it to hot chocolate, too. The* *interplay between the falernum and the orgeat is interesting in this drink, and although calvados is called for, I should add that the drink works well with Laird's Bottled-in-Bond applejack, too.*

Bâton Rouge

Adapted from a recipe by
Julien Escot,
Papa Doble, Montpellier, France.

"A tribute to the popular Vieux Carré Cocktail."
—Julien Escot.

1 dash Peychaud's bitters

1 dash Angostura bitters

20 ml (.66 oz) sweet vermouth

20 ml (.66 oz) Xanté cognac pear liqueur

20 ml (.66 oz) cognac V.S.O.P.

20 ml (.66 oz) amber rum

1 long lemon twist, as garnish

Stir over ice and strain into a chilled cocktail glass. Add
the garnish.

gaz sez: *I love this twist on the Vieux Carré. Rum
and cognac always play nice together, so that's a
natural twist on the original rye and cognac, but
it's the Xanté cognac pear liqueur that makes this
drink stand up to be counted. It's a fabulous product, and it's brought into play brilliantly here by
M. Escot. Bon travail, Julien!*

Bollywood

Adapted from a recipe by
**Kathy Casey,
Liquid Kitchen**, Seattle, WA.

"I created this exotic libation for the Chameleon Club at the Abu Dhabi Fairmont in the UAE. I wanted to pull together all the influences and flavors of the area, from the curry, coconut, mint, and rose to the gold bling to the love of Bollywood. It has a lot of ingredients and prep, but is worth the effort."
—Kathy Casey.

2 large fresh mint sprigs

45 ml (1.5 oz) Tanqueray No. TEN gin

60 ml (2 oz) Bollywood Pre-Mix*

Coconut Rose Foam**, as garnish

Edible gold flakes, as garnish

Tear mint and drop into a pint glass. Add ice and the remaining ingredients. Shake vigorously and strain into a chilled cocktail glass. Top with a pouf of Coconut Rose Foam and garnish with sprinkle of gold.

***Bollywood Pre-Mix**: Combine 400 g (2 cups) sugar, 480 ml (2 cups) water, and 1/2 tablespoon good curry powder in a small saucepan and bring to a simmer. Remove from heat and let sit for 20 minutes. Strain and discard solids, then cool completely. Stir in 720 ml (3 cups) fresh lime juice and 480 ml (2 cups) fresh pineapple juice. Transfer to a clean bottle and store in the refrigerator.

Coconut Rose Foam: Place 2 gelatin sheets in a bowl of ice water and "bloom" (soak till soft) for about 10 minutes. Combine 90 ml (3 oz) Monin Rose Syrup, 60 ml (2 oz) fresh lemon juice, 60 ml (2 oz) water and 90 ml (3 oz) simple syrup, then strain through a fine strainer into a small saucepan. Remove gelatin from ice water, squeeze out excess water, and add to saucepan. Heat over medium-high heat just until gelatin is dissolved. Immediately remove the saucepan from the heat. Do not boil. Stir in 240 ml (8 oz) canned unsweetened coconut milk. Let cool 10 minutes (set a timer). Pour mixture into a whipped cream canister. Charge with two NO2 charger cartridges and *immediately* shake well. Refrigerate at least 4 hours or overnight. Shake well upside down before discharging foam onto cocktail. Store in refrigerator for up to 4 to 5 days. Makes 1 canister of foam.

gaz sez: *Jeez, Kathy, you're so darned geeky! Okay, I'll admit it, I didn't test this one, but I know Kathy Casey well enough to know that she don't submit rotten recipes, and I also wanted to have a few examples of just how far some people out there are pushing the envelope. Unfortunately, only those people who really understand ingredients can pull this sort of drink off. Fortunately, Kathy is such a person.*

Brigadoon

Adapted from a recipe by
Adam James McGurk,
Hawksmoor, Seven Dials, London, UK.

"The intention behind this drink was to create an accessible drink to introduce people to scotch. The 10-year-old Glenmorangie works well as it is, in itself, an accessible whisky, light and fruity. But it can work well with others, as the ingredients showcase all light fruity styles well and work great with richer sherry notes found whiskies such as Glenfarclas 12-year-old. The addition of orgeat was a natural choice as both almonds and apricots are drupes (stone fruit). The drink shares its name with the book and musical set in Scotland, which tells of a mysterious blessed town that appears for just one day once every 100 years."
—Adam James McGurk.

5 ml (.17 oz) orgeat

15 ml (.5 oz) fresh lemon juice

20 ml (.66 oz) apricot brandy

45 ml (1.5 oz) Glenmorangie Original scotch whisky

1 orange twist, as garnish

Shake over ice and strain into a chilled coupette or cocktail glass, or over cubed ice in a rocks glass. Add the garnish.

gaz sez: *Nice and simple, and simply fabulous. I love Glenmorangie—it was the first single malt distillery I ever visited (1992) and I have very warm memories of that trip. Thanks, Anthony. Thanks, Alex.*

Broken English

Adapted from a recipe by
Colin Shearn,
The Franklin Mortgage & Investment Co.,
Philadelphia, PA.

60 ml (2 oz) Beefeater 24 gin

30 ml (1 oz) sweet vermouth

15 ml (.5 oz) Strega

7.5 ml (.25 oz) Fernet Branca

1 teaspoon Bénédictine

2 dashes Regans' Orange Bitters No. 6

2 dashes Peychaud's bitters

1 grapefruit twist, as garnish

Stir over ice and strain into a chilled cocktail glass. Add
the garnish.

gaz sez: *I must say that I like the name of this
one. Reminds me of one of my all-time fave albums
by Marianne Faithfull. There's an absolutely filthy
track on there called Why'd Ya Do It. Check it out.*

*As for the drink, well, this one is just plain weird.
But it works so darned well. Beefeater 24 plus
sweet vermouth make sense, right? Adding Strega
isn't that much of a stretch, either. But to then
add Fernet AND Bénédictine AND orange bitters AND Peychaud's bitters, well, it doesn't make
much sense on paper, but it sure as hell works well
in a glass. This is one of those recipes in which measuring ingredients properly is essential—and bear
in mind that I'm a free-pourer of long standing.*

221

One slip of the hand on this one, though, and the whole thing falls down and goes bump. Build it properly and you get a whole symphony orchestra playing Tchaikovsky's 1812 in your mouth. There are cannons exploding here, kettle drums pounding over there, and cymbals crashing all over the place. Colin Shearn sure as hell has a weird brain, though... .

Brown Bitter Stirred

Adapted from a recipe by
**Jason Schiffer,
320 Main**, Seal Beach, CA.

"Drink through the mouth… ."
—Jason Schiffer.

60 ml (2 oz) Russell's Reserve 6 year old rye whiskey

15 ml (.5 oz) Cynar

15 ml (.5 oz) Carpano Antica

7.5 ml (.25 oz) Clément Créole Shrubb

2 dashes The Bitter Truth Old Time Aromatic bitters

1 orange twist

1 lemon twist, as garnish

Stir over ice and strain into a chilled cocktail glass.
Squeeze the orange twist over the drink and rub around
the outside of the glass (not the rim), then discard.
Squeeze and rub the lemon twist, then add to the drink.

gaz sez: *This is a pretty peculiar potion, and I was surprised at how well the Cynar and the Carpano played off each other, but it's the Russell's Reserve that commands the glass in this baby. It's a beautiful whiskey that brings everything else in this recipe together in harmony. They're singing "My Old Kentucky Home."*

Cardarita

Adapted from a recipe by
**Agostino Perrone,
Connaught Bar**, London, UK.

"It is a sort of cross of a cardamom Margarita and Paloma. The Almond Cardamom Sugar recipe is from Simone Maci, Fresco Bar, Como, Italy."—Agostino Perrone.

50 ml (1.65 oz) Calle 23 blanco tequila

15 ml (.5 oz) Almond Cardamom Sugar*

100 ml (3.32 oz) fresh pink grapefruit juice

15 ml (.5 oz) Galliano L'Autentico

20 ml (.66 oz) ginger ale

1 grapefruit twist, as garnish

Shake over ice and strain into a tall ice-filled glass. Top with ginger ale. Flame the twist over the drink, then add as garnish.

*Almond Cardamom Sugar: Combine 250 g sweet almonds (no shell), 125 g caster or super-fine sugar, 18 oz sugar syrup, . 4 oz water, 4 cardamom pods, grated nutmeg (1/4 of a whole one). Place all the ingredients in the food processor and blend. Filter only 1 time to keep some of the texture. Store in fridge.

gaz sez: *I love Ago's style. The first time I met him he fixed me what was perhaps the best Martinez I ever did drink. Disclaimer: Ago does some Ambassador work for Galliano. That said, it's the Galliano L'Autentico that lifts this drink from the ranks of a refreshing quaff and promotes it to the stroke-of-genius category. It's almost as though Ago used the Galliano as a form of bitters in this drink—it brings all the other ingredients together in harmony, and adds layers and layers of flavors all its own.*

The Cinquecento

Adapted from a recipe by
**Fredo Ceraso,
Loungerati.com**, Brooklyn, NY.

"In April 2010, I submitted this original cocktail to the Louis 649 bar for their Anyone Can Be a Mixologist contest. It won first place and a place on their menu. Some background: This cocktail is called the Cinquecento (500 in Italian) to honor the two modifying spirits: DOM Bénédictine (celebrating its 500th anniversary) and Campari (which hails from Torino, home of the iconic Fiat Cinquecento). Campari is a natural mixer with grapefruit juice. The vodka acts as the engine for this cocktail which is meant to be an *aperitivo*. In other words, DOM meets MOD, a drink that you could have in Torino or West London or Brooklyn. Brad Farran, head bartender at Clover Club, told me this it is his "go-to" cocktail when someone insists on a vodka cocktail. It will also be featured on the cocktail menu of the Blythswood Square Hotel bar in Glasgow by award winning mixologist Mal Spence."
—Fredo Ceraso.

45 ml (1.5 oz) Luksusowa vodka

15 ml (.5 oz) Bénédictine

15 ml (.5 oz) Campari

22.5 ml (.75 oz) fresh grapefruit juice

2 dashes Angostura bitters

1 grapefruit twist, as garnish

Shake vigorously over ice and double-strain into a
chilled coupe. Add the garnish.

225

gaz sez: *Well Fredo kinda took my job away from me on this one—he describes the drink well. I will add, though, that it's really nice to see vodka being used in a recipe that's well thought out.*

Coral Reef

Adapted from a recipe by
**Lyn Farmer,
Silversea Cruises**, Miami, FL.

"This drink was created for the Silver Twists on the Classics cocktail menu of Silversea Cruises as a loose takeoff on the Negroni. It was named by a guest, who admired the luminous orange color and said it was just like coral."
—Lyn Farmer.

60 ml (2 oz) Plymouth gin

30 ml (1 oz) St. Germain

22.5 ml (.75 oz) Aperol

Club soda

1 lemon twist, as garnish

Build in a highball glass over ice. Add the garnish.

gaz sez: *Elegantly simple, and simply fabulous. This one works very well without the club soda, too. Nice work, Lyn.*

227

Cortez the Killer

Adapted from a recipe by
Brent Butler,
Blackbird, San Francisco, CA.

After we notified Brent that his cocktail had been selected for the 101 Best New Cocktails list, he wrote, "There has been one alteration to the cocktail that I have implemented that you can choose whether or not to include in the book. I have been making batches of Cortez the Killer and aging them for four weeks in a Hudson rye barrel, delicious!" Sounds like a plan.

60 ml (2 oz) Lunazul blanco tequila

22.5 ml (.75 oz) Bonal aperitif wine*

7.5 ml (.25 oz) crème de cacao

1 small orange twist, as garnish

Stir over ice for 15 seconds and strain into a chilled coupe. Add the garnish.

*Bonal (from Alpenz web site): Since 1865, this delicious aperitif wine has stood apart for its exceptional complexity, delightful flavors and stimulating palate. Serious to its role as aperitif, it was known as "ouvre l'appétit" - the key to the appetite. Found popular with sportsmen, Bonal became an early sponsor of the Tour de France. It is made by an infusion of gentian, cinchona (quinine) and renown herbs of the Grand Chartreuse mountains in a Mistelle base. Traditionally enjoyed neat or with a twist; also may enhance classic drinks in place of sweet red vermouth.

gaz sez: *I'm writing about these drinks out of alpha-order, and since this one begins with a C it might be the first recipe you see that brings a tiny amount of crème de cacao into play. I guarantee you that it won't be the last. It works well if you deal the cards right, too, and here it plays a distant drum that marks the beat for the Bonal. This is a fabulous drink.*

Decolletage

Adapted from a recipe by
Chris Hannah,
French 75 Bar, New Orleans, LA.

"When I first heard the word decolletage spoken aloud I was dazzled … and then after discovering its meaning I was enchanted. I was determined to create a cocktail worthy of its name—enjoy."
—Chris Hannah.

45 ml (1.5 oz) El Tesoro reposado tequila

30 ml (1 oz) Dubonnet Rouge

15 ml (.5 oz) Aperol

7.5 ml (.25 oz) Fernet Branca

1 orange twist, as garnish

Stir over ice and strain into an ice-filled brandy snifter
(or double old-fashioned glass). Break the twist over the
drink, then add as garnish.

gaz sez: *Chris gets extra points for being "determined to create a cocktail worthy of" the name decolletage, He's a man after my own heart. His creativity, which has been widely, and deservedly, acknowledged in the cocktail community, is shown off with shiny brass buttons in this drink. It's a Decolletage that teases to the point of the areolae. The tequila, Dubonnet, and Aperol all make sense in terms of pretty much knowing that they'll play nice together in the sand box, but then the Fernet comes along and the bar is automatically raised. Will it commend the glass? And the answer is no. It adds layers and layers of complexity, but it also allows all the other ingredients play their part. Nice one, Chris.*

Desmo

Adapted from a recipe by
Bradford Scott Knutson,
Swing Wine Bar, Olympia, WA.

"The subtle sweetness of aged balsamic pairs superbly with the cognac, while simultaneously cutting just a little of its heat … [and] the flavor of the balsamic merely makes a great liquor even greater. I made this for a customer who enjoyed it so much I let him name the drink. He was a rep for Ducati motorcycles and named it Desmo after the engine. Variations: Not everyone can get their hands on aged balsamic, a readily available substitution would be to make your own balsamic reduction. Although the aged product creates a subtle smoothness that a reduction cannot duplicate, this would only be noted when tasted side by side."
—Bradford Scott Knutson.

4 to 6 drops well-aged balsamic vinegar (Bradford used
a 50-year-old Italian bottling)

45 ml (1.5 oz) high-quality cognac

Add the vinegar and the cognac to a brandy snifter, and
swirl the glass to combine the ingredients.

gaz sez: *At last—a simple and very successful way of incorporating balsamic vinegar into a mixed drink. This drink makes for very interesting sipping, and of course it changes drastically depending on which cognac you use. Pierre Ferrand Abel stands up to the vinegar very well indeed, as does Martell Cordon Bleu, and Hennessy XO—my*

231

fave bottling in the Hennessy line. I also liked this drink made with Courvoisier XO, Hardy XO, and Hine XO Antique. Many thanks to Pete and Sal at Painter's for letting me raid their stash!

Dilettante's Punch

Adapted from a recipe by
**Ms. Franky Marshall,
The Clover Club**, New York City, NY.

"The Dilettante's Punch is a versatile potable. The rich flavor makes some think of Christmas and fireplaces; yet the combination of red wine and pêche over ice can easily transport one to a *terrazza* for al fresco sipping. It can also be served as a punch bowl for a group (specs on request), or served

233

warm. In addition, this cocktail can be made easily and
quickly. Voila!"

—Franky Marshall.

90 ml (3 oz) dry red wine with medium to full body (such
as Chianti or Cabernet Sauvignon)

15 ml (.5 oz) Smith & Cross rum

15 ml (.5 oz) Mathilde pêche

15 ml (.5 oz) demerara syrup (1:1)

15 ml (.5 oz) fresh lemon juice

1 dash The Bitter Truth Jerry Thomas' Own Decanter
bitters

1 lemon wheel, as garnish

1 toasted cinnamon stick, as garnish

Build in a wine glass. Add cobbled ice and stir (to perfection). Add the garnishes and two straws so that they
are half-immersed in the cocktail.

gaz sez: *I love the way Ms. Franky has approached
this drink, using wine as the base and peppering it
with lots of different nuances. It's a veritable gala
in a glass.*

Dirt 'n' Diesel

Adapted from a recipe by
Cale Green,
Tavern Law/Needle & Thread, Seattle, A.

This recipe was included in *GQ* magazine's recent feature on the 25 best cocktail bars in America.

60 ml (2 oz) Cruzan Black Strap rum

15 ml (.5 oz) Fernet Branca

15 ml (.5 oz) demerara syrup

7.5 ml (.25 oz) Cynar

7.5 ml (.25 oz) fresh lime juice

1 lime wedge, as garnish

Shake over ice and strain into a chilled cocktail coupe.

Add the garnish. Smile.

gaz sez: *My, oh my. I quite honestly didn't like the look of this recipe when I was eyeballing it, and I almost didn't bother to test it at all, but something about it kept making me think again about Dirt 'n' Diesel, I think it was probably the Fernet. Anyway, when I did get around to taking this baby around the dance floor, I was very happy to be proved wrong about the formula. And I love that sneaky hint of lime juice that dances at the back of the throat.*

Division Bell

Adapted from a recipe by
Philip Ward,
Mayahuel, New York City.

30 ml (1 oz) Del Maguey Mezcal San Luis del Rio

22.5 ml (.75 oz) Aperol

15 ml (.5 oz) Luxardo maraschino liqueur

22.5 ml (.75 oz) fresh lime juice

1 grapefruit twist

Shake over ice and strain into a chilled cocktail glass.

Squeeze the twist over the drink, then discard.

gaz sez: *Okay, so I love Phil Ward and I can't resist including one of his recipes in this batch. Sue me, already. Then make this cocktail and tell me it ain't absolutely fabulous. The balance is perfect, every ingredient plays a discernable role, and the grapefruit twist caps it off beautifully.*

The Double "D"

Adapted from a recipe by
Dale DeGroff,
New York City, NY.

This autumnal martini-style cocktail brings Double Cross vodka and Dale DeGroff together in its name.

60 ml (2 oz) Double Cross vodka

7.5 ml (.25 oz) Pear Elixir*

1 dash Dale DeGroff's Pimento bitters

Miniature bottled pear, as garnish**

Stir over ice and strain into a cocktail glass. Place the pear garnish on a cocktail pick in the bottom of the glass.

Pear Elixir: Mix together 2 parts Maraska Kruskovac pear brandy, 1 part Mathilde Liqueur Poires, and 1/50 part Westford Hill Distillers (Ashford, Conn.) pear William eau de vie.

**Available through Double Cross Vodka (www.doublecrossvodka.com) for free.

gaz sez: *Dale sent us this recipe at the very last minute, and he swore that by the time this book was actually on the shelves the Double Cross vodka people would have miniature bottled pear garnishes available for free from their web site, and his pimiento bitters would be available, too. I sure hope he was right... .*

El Dorado de Pizarro

Adapted from a recipe by
**Robert Hearne,
Grape Street Underground,**
Denver, CO.

"Created and paired well with the arrival of fall weather.
Named for the legendary city of gold and the conquistador
who never found it."
—Robert Hearne.

60 ml (2 oz) Hacienda de Chihuahua Sotol Plata

30 ml (1 oz) fresh lime juice

30 ml (1 oz) Grand Marnier

1 teaspoon Averna amaro

2 dashes Bittermens Xocolatl Mole bitters

1 small pinch salt

1 lime wedge, as garnish

Shake over ice and strain into a chilled cocktail glass (preferably one with blue or green glass and a hand-blown, South-of-the-Border look). Add the garnish.

gaz sez: *Sotol as a base spirit! What a brave soul is Robert Hearne. He pulls it off, too. The Grand Marnier serves to soften, the Averno leaps up and grabs your attention, the bitters round the drink out, and the pinch of salt seals the deal. Nice crafted, Robert.*

When I wrote to Robert to tell him that his drink was going to be included here, he got back to me to fess up that he wasn't a professional bartender, but I couldn't bring myself to take this drink out of the list. It's one of the perks of writing your own rules.

239

El Oso

Adapted from a recipe by
**Brendan Dorr,
B&O American Brasserie**,
Baltimore, MD.

"This is the winner of the 2010 US National Barenjager
Cocktail Competition. The judges called it 'a perfectly balanced cocktail that highlighted Barenjager beautifully and
created an instant classic.'"
——Brendan Dorr.

52.5 ml (1.75 oz) Partida añejo tequila

22.5 ml (.75 oz) Barenjager honey liqueur

15 ml (.5 oz) Luxardo maraschino liqueur

2 dashes The Bitter Truth Jerry Thomas' Own Decanter
bitters

1 dried orange wheel, as garnish

1 Kold-Draft ice cube, as garnish

Combine all ingredients in a mixing glass, add ice, and
stir 40 times. Place the orange wheel in a large rocks
glass, add the ice cube, and strain. ¡Salud!

gaz sez: *I was one of the judges at this competition,
so the El Oso was an obvious drink to include in
this year's 101 Best New Cocktails. It's well crafted,
well balanced, and well, it glides down the throat
with the greatest of ease. Nice one, Brendan.*

Fear and Loathing in Princeton

Adapted from a recipe by
**Mattias Hagglund,
elements**, Princeton, NJ.

"Buy the ticket, take the ride."—Hunter S. Thompson.

60 ml (2 oz) Hayman's Old Tom gin

22.5 ml (.75 oz) Campari

15 ml (.5 oz) Averna amaro

15 ml (.5 oz) agave nectar

1 barspoon Del Maguey Mezcal Vida

1 orange twist, as garnish

Hard-shake and double-strain into a chilled cocktail
glass. Flame the twist over the drink, then rub it around
the rim of the glass. Drop it in and serve or (better)
imbibe.

gaz sez: *Here's another crazy-looking formula that turns out to be a very well-balanced drink. I'm intrigued by the use of mezcal in very small quantities that I've seen in more than a couple of drinks submitted this year. Not all of them worked well, but this one certainly did.*

Thanks for giving me the chance to grow. Couldn't have done it without you guys.

Fig and Sage Smash

Adapted from a recipe by
Jamie Walsh,
Stoddard's Fine Food & Ale,
Boston, MA.

"A fun cocktail that doesn't go with the trendy mint and basil thing…. People should look for using more variety of herbs, like dill, marjoram, lavender, oregano, rosemary, summer savory, and thyme. Tarragon is my favorite in gin or tequila. I will use fresh ginger with egg white, tarragon and tequila…. Poor tequila, it gets no love."
—Jamie Walsh.

1 fig

3 sage leaves

60 ml (2 oz) Knob Creek bourbon

15 ml (.5 oz) orange curaçao

22.5 ml (.75 oz) fresh lemon juice

1 barspoon Bénédictine

Slice the fig and reserve 1 piece as garnish. Muddle the remaining fig and 2 sage leaves (reserve 1 leaf as garnish) in a mixing glass. Add the remaining ingredients and crushed ice. Shake and strain into a chilled double old-fashioned glass. Add the garnishes.

gaz sez: *Here comes the sage thing again, and this boy loves his sage. It's very interesting to see how prettily the fig plays with sage, too. I'd never have dreamed of putting those two together in a glass, but here they are, and the result is pretty astonishing.*

First Class

Adapted from a recipe by
Frank Caiafa,
Peacock Alley Restaurant,
New York City, NY.

"I was saving this cocktail for the G'Vine competition but after completing the exam, I didn't realize that there was an extensive essay portion. Unfortunately, my duties here at Peacock Alley, coupled with the closing stages of finishing my band's new album, leaves little time for dissertations of any kind. Maybe I'll be able to go all-in next year."
—Frank Caiafa.

4 fresh sage leaves*

1 lime wedge

15 ml (.5 oz) fresh lime juice

75 ml (2.5 oz) G'Vine Floraison gin

30 ml (1 oz) Luxardo maraschino liqueur

Freshly ground black pepper, as garnish

Muddle the sage, lime, and lime juice in a mixing glass. Add the ice and remaining ingredients. Shake and strain into a chilled cocktail glass. Add the garnish.

* It is very important to clean the sage leaves.

gaz sez: *I love sage. I love sage and onion stuffing and I love burning sage to cleanse the house, and I love the sage in this drink, too. It not only plays very nicely with the G'Vine Floraison (a fabulously floral, New Western style gin from France), the sage also works really well with the highly perfumed Luxardo maraschino, too. And the ground*

245

black pepper garnish gives the First Class cocktail its crowning glory—it's a garnish that adds yet one more dimension to this drink. Frank's a very creative guy.

Flor de Jerez

Adapted from a recipe by
**Joaquin Simo,
Death & Co.**,
New York City, NY.

"I wanted to come up with a drier aperitif cocktail that still had some bright fruitiness. Amontillado sherry isn't as delicate as manzanilla, so I knew it could stand up to a base spirit being used as a modifier. I always get a big dried apricot note from the Appleton Reserve, so I echoed that note with the fresh fruit taste of Orchard apricot liqueur. Toasted almond notes and spice notes abound, and the drink stays dry due to the double dose of acidity between the sherry and lemon juice. A great example of a low-abv cocktail that doesn't skimp on taste or complexity."

—Joaquin Simo.

45 ml (1.5 oz) Lustau Los Arcos amontillado sherry

15 ml (.5 oz) Appleton Estate Reserve rum

22.5 ml (.75 oz) fresh lemon juice

15 ml (.5 oz) Petite Canne Sugar Cane syrup

7.5 ml (.25 oz) Orchard apricot liqueur

1 dash Angostura bitters

Shake over ice and strain into chilled port glass or cocktail glass.

gaz sez: *A true cocktailian mind is at work here, and since I know Joaquin pretty well, I'm not in the least bit surprised to see that he's come up with*

247

something that's completely original. This drink is like a first-class orgy—everyone is playing with someone else, and everyone comes at the same time. It's an explosion in a glass.

Flying Peppa

Adapted from a recipe by
**Olivier Jacobs,
Cafe Theatre**,
Gent, Belgium.

"This is actually a variation (as you probably will have noticed) on the Aviation, where the pepper works really well with the crème de violette. Depending on the crème de violette you use, you can change the proportions, violette can have an overwhelming taste if used too vigorously. As for the maraschino, I prefer using Maraska, it hasn't got the strong taste like the Luxardo but that's just what makes it work so good in this drink, not overwhelming but more working together. Enjoy!"
—Olivier Jacobs.

1/4 yellow bell pepper

50 ml (1.65 oz) Tanqueray No. TEN gin (Geranium
works really nice as well)

20 ml (.66 oz) Maraska maraschino liqueur

15 ml (.5 oz) crème de violette

20 ml (.66 oz) fresh lemon juice

1 nice cherry, as garnish (please don't use the cheap
maraschino ones)

Muddle the pepper in a mixing glass. Add ice and the
remaining ingredients. Shake vigorously (I love this
word) and double-strain into a chilled cocktail glass.
Add the garnish, smile, and don't let it have the time to
get warm.

gaz sez: *I admit that I used Luxardo maraschino
when I tested this one, and I used Crème Yvette for*

249

the violette, too, but the drink turned out to be fabulous, and I just loved the way in which the pepper added an extra dimension to the drink without detracting too very much from the other ingredients.

The Foxtail

Adapted from a recipe by
**Thomas Kunick,
Rumor Lounge**,
Las Vegas, NV.

"This drink was created to promote Oxley gin at an event at the Downtown Cocktail Room in Las Vegas. It has also been recently featured in *Vegas Seven* magazine, a local publication, honoring Bénédictine."
—Thomas Kunick.

30 ml (1 oz) Oxley gin

30 ml (1 oz) Bénédictine

30 ml (1 oz) white grapefruit juice

1 grapefruit twist, as garnish

Shake over ice and strain into a chilled cocktail glass.
Squeeze the twist over the drink, then add as garnish.

gaz sez: *White grapefruit juice and Bénédictine go so damned well together you're not going to believe how good this drink is until you taste it for yourself. The Oxley gin ain't too shabby in the Foxtail, either. It bravely makes itself known as the overlord of the other two ingredients, but it lets them strut their own stuff, too. Nicely done, Thomas.*

251

Ghost in the Graveyard

Adapted from a recipe by
**Jane Lopes,
The Violet Hour**,
Chicago, IL.

"The Violet Hour, recently named the #3 bar in the country by *GQ* magazine, is a cocktail bar that focuses on crafting well-balanced classic cocktails and variations thereon. The bar only permits enough people in as there are seats for, allowing us to provide time-consuming, detail-oriented cocktails and a relaxed experience to our customers."
—Jane Lopes.

30 ml (1 oz) Cocchi Americano*

30 ml (1 oz) yellow Chartreuse

30 ml (1 oz) Amaro Montenegro

30 ml (1 oz) fresh lime juice

1 mint sprig, as garnish

Shake over ice and strain into an old-fashioned glass with fresh ice. Add the garnish.

*"This aperitivo – something along the lines of a vermouth – has been made since 1891 from moscato d'Asti, a sweet white wine fortified with a touch of brandy, then flavored with gentian, cinchona bark and other bittering aromatics, along with orange peels and herbs. There are any number of similar products on the market, but what has cocktail enthusiasts excited about Cocchi is that it is secretly acknowledged to be the most similar product in existence to the old-formula Kina Lillet." Toby Cecchini, **New York Times**, April 21, 2010.

gaz sez: *Jane Lopes is one brave bartender. This drink took guts to create, and how Jane came to even dream about putting these ingredients together in a glass is completely beyond me, but the drink is just fabulous. My hat's off to Jane Lopes.*

Golden Dog

Adapted from a recipe by
**Matt Piacentini,
'inoteca liquori bar**,
New York City, NY.

"Very light and ethereal, the apricot and smoke of the Talisker seem to dance in the air over a soft bed of rich and deep earthy undertones. If you want to make it a little richer, say on a cold night, substitute the Lillet with Bonal. Please resist the urge to stir. The flavors won't blend."
—Matt Piacentini.

45 ml (1.5 oz) Talisker 10 Year Old scotch whisky

15 ml (.5 oz) Rothman & Winter orchard apricot liqueur

15 ml (.5 oz) Lillet Blanc

15 ml (.5 oz) Bénédictine

Shake over ice and strain into a chilled cocktail glass.

gaz sez: *I'm a sucker for Talisker so I couldn't wait to get my hands on this number. I trotted down to Painter's, my local in the Hudson Valley, got behind the stick in their Gallery bar, which is used only on special occasions, and put this one together just a couple of days after receiving the recipe. Then I made a second one and got Pete Buttiglieri, one of the two brothers who owns the joint and a great friend of mine, to join me. We had a grand old afternoon. Nice drink, Matt.*

Golden Promise

Adapted from a recipe by
**James Connolly,
Defectors**,
Perth, Australia.

"A twist on a Sazerac, using the grassy notes of The Macallan to work with the thyme syrup. Its floral nose also ties in well with the elderflower liqueur, and the Peychaud's bitters ties it all together."
—James Connolly.

5 ml (.17 oz) St. Germain, as rinse

5 ml (.17 oz) Thyme Syrup*

3 dashes Peychaud's bitters

60 ml (2 oz) The Macallan 12 Years Old scotch whisky

1 lemon twist

Rinse a chilled cocktail glass with the St. Germain; set aside. Stir the remaining ingredients over ice and strain into the glass. Squeeze the twist over the drink, then discard.

***Thyme Syrup**: Combine 150 ml (5 oz) of sugar syrup (1:1) with 10 g (1 teaspoon) finely chopped thyme in a whipped cream canister. Charge with 2 nitrogen cartridges and shake for 1 minute. Release gas slowly and fine-strain into desired vessel.

gaz sez: *This drink is all over the place, and I think that James made a wise choice when he picked The Macallan as his base—it's a solid enough bottling to keep the other flavors—thyme, elderflower and Peychaud's, no less—under control. This is a complex dram with a very sturdy backbone.*

255

Gran Woodford

Adapted from a recipe by
Steve Quezada,
Boston, MA.

"After a few tweaks, this recipe turned out the most balanced. I tried Navan in place of the Dolin, but found it not
as balanced or smooth. My testers agreed. I hope you will
too. Cheers."
—Steve Quezada.

1 ripe black mission fig

5 drops Bittermens Xocolatl Mole bitters

60 ml (2 oz) Woodford Reserve bourbon

15 ml (.5 oz) Gran Gala

15 ml (.5 oz) Dolin Rouge vermouth

1 cherry, as garnish

Muddle the fig and bitters in a mixing glass. Add ice and
the remaining ingredients. Shake vigorously and strain
into a chilled cocktail glass. Add the garnish.

gaz sez: *Figs and mole bitters! A marriage made in
heaven! I almost gave this one a standing ovation.
Need I say more?*

Grapefruit Whistlestop

PART 4 • OTHER PEOPLE'S STUFF

Adapted from a recipe by
**Hannah Lanfear,
GloGlo's**,
London, UK.

"The Grapefruit Whistlestop is a lightly alcoholic cocktail, making it a perfect brunchtime cocktail and is very refreshing."
—Hannah Lanfear.

40 ml (1.33 oz) Aperol

20 ml (.66 oz) Tio Pepe

15 ml (.5 oz) fresh lemon juice

10 ml (.33 oz) honey syrup

20 ml (.66 oz) fresh pink grapefruit juice

1 pink grapefruit twist

Shake over ice and fine-strain into a chilled coupette.
Apply a spray of pink grapefruit oil to the rim of the
coupette from the twist (for aroma but not bitterness),
then discard.

gaz sez: *Like a freshly-picked bunch of wildflowers, this one dances all over the place. I love the way the Aperol and sherry play nice with each other here, and the grapefruit juice (and oils) makes for a great sandbox, too.*

The Greatest Generation

Adapted from a recipe by
Francis Schott,
The Cocktail Bar at Catherine Lombardi,
New Brunswick, NJ.

"I sent you a submission for your upcoming list of cocktails (and bartenders). I hope I am eligible for consideration for both as I do get behind the stick at my own place still."
—Francis Schott.

22.5 ml (.75 oz) Hennessy VS cognac

22.5 ml (.75 oz) Bénédictine

22.5 ml (.75 oz) Cointreau

7.5 ml (.25 oz) Aperol

45 ml (1.5 oz) Mumm Cordon Rouge champagne

Peychaud's bitters, as garnish

Stir all ingredients except champagne over ice. Strain into a chilled champagne flute and top with champagne. Float a several dashes bitters on top to make a very small collar around the top of the flute.

gaz sez: *Here's an interesting mix of ingredients, right? I get the Cointreau and Bénédictine playing nice with each other, but I was afraid that the Aperol would start a fight in the glass. I was wrong. This is a fabulous drink.*

His & Hers

PART 4 • OTHER PEOPLE'S STUFF

Adapted from a recipe for Valentine's Day by
**Owen Westman,
The Rickhouse**,
San Francisco, CA
(currently owner of **The Collection Bar**,
Melbourne, Australia).

"Alas, in life we are faced with an array decisions, some of which have actual bearing on the course of our travels, and the destinies for which we live. But ease thy heart, because this is not one of them ... for within each option lies enough exhilaration and fire to deliver balance to even the most lovesick amongst us."
—Rickhouse Cocktail Menu, February, 2010.

45 ml (1.5 oz) Plymouth gin or Russell's Reserve Rye whiskey

15 ml (.5 oz) Bénédictine

7.5 ml (.25 oz) yellow Chartreuse

2 dashes house bitters

3 dashes raspberry eau de vie, as an aromatic garnish

Stir over ice and strain into a chilled champagne coupe.

Top with 3 dashes raspberry eau de vie.

gaz sez: *I love the fact that this drink can be made with either gin or whiskey. I did something similar in 2009 when, at a MOTAC event, I came up with the Plymouth Hoe (Plymouth gin, Grand Marnier, Navan vanilla liqueur, and Angostura), and then used the same formula substituting Mak-*

259

er's Mark for the gin. Worked perfectly. The real genius in the His & Hers, though, lies in the raspberry eau de vie aromatic garnish. It adds dimension to drink that, because of the two very complex liqueurs called for, already has a lot going for it. Nice one, Owen.

Hound of the Baskervilles

Adapted from a recipe by
**Michael J. Neff,
Ward III**,
New York City, NY.

4 cucumber slices

1 pinch lapsang souchong tea leaves

7.5 ml (.25 oz) green Chartreuse VEP

7.5 ml (.25 oz) Dolin sweet vermouth

75 ml (2.5 oz)

3 cucumber slices, as garnish

Muddle the cucumber and tea in a mixing glass. Add ice
and the remaining ingredients. Stir and double-strain
into a chilled rocks glass over two ice cubes. Add the
garnish.

gaz sez: *I had a very pleasant evening at Ward III in late 2010. It went on until the wee hours. I misbehaved. 'nuff said. Michael's use of tea and cucumbers in this drink is interesting since he didn't go for the obvious base spirit—Hendrick's—but instead he chose the most fabulous Red Breast Pot Still Irish whiskey. Nice touch, Michael. And the vermouth and the Chartreuse in this drink both add subtle textures to the finished product. I could probably drink two of these... .*

The Ice Pick

Adapted from a recipe by
**Daniel Eun,
The Varnish**,
Los Angeles, CA.

60 ml (2 oz) Bols Genever

7.5 ml (.25 oz) crème de violette

7.5 ml (.25 oz) Maraska maraschino liqueur

2 dashes Regans' Orange Bitters No. 6

1 lemon twist, as garnish

Stir over ice and strain over a large rock in a rocks glass.
Add the garnish.

gaz sez: *Dan-yul really knows his stuff. He's proved
it time and time again. He's a brave bartender, too,
as you can see by this recipe. Nice one, Mr. Eun.*

In a Pickle

Adapted from a recipe by
**Ted Kilgore,
Taste by Niche**,
Saint Louis, MO.

"I created this cocktail because I had a guest request something that tasted like a pickle. It then became my best-selling cocktail."
—Ted Kilgore.

2 cucumber slices

1 small dill sprig

45 ml (1.5 oz) Hendrick's gin

15 ml (.5 oz) Velvet Falernum

15 ml (.5 oz) St. Germain

22.5 ml (.75 oz) fresh lime juice

1 cucumber slice, as garnish

1 small dill sprig, as garnish

Muddle the cucumber and dill in a mixing glass. Add ice and the remaining ingredients. Shake vigorously for 20 seconds and strain into an ice-filled highball glass (I use one large cube). Rub the rim of the glass with the cucumber slice, then lay the cucumber gently on top of the drink. "Spank" the dill sprig, then set it on top of the cucumber slice. Serve with a short straw and an impish grin.

gaz sez: *Ted's my favorite crazy bastard bartender. There, I've said it. What impresses me most about his drinks is his flexibility. Most of his creations tend toward the strong, Manhattan-like twists*

263

on classics, though he takes the twists to extremes at times. Then, when you're least expecting it, he comes up with a dainty little number like this drink, and the cocktail turns out to be as smooth as a finely-tuned Harley. Let's say that this is Ted showing us his feminine side, huh?

I Say Bombay, You Say Mumbai

Adapted from a recipe by
Tim Etherington-Judge,
Taj Mahal Palace Hotel,
Mumbai, India.

"This drink is served in two parts, each a half-sized portion. The city with two names spawns a twist with two flavours: Bombay—old colonial bastion of the British Raj from a time when the sweet vermouth'd Martinez was the martini of choice and gin was de rigueur. Mumbai—the hustling, bustling home of Indian fashionistas, Bollywood megastars, and the corporate elite where today's trend is tomorrow's passé."
— Tim Etherington-Judge.

Bombay

15 ml (.5 oz) Bombay Sapphire gin (when in Rome, as they say)

15 ml (.5 oz) Masala Sweet Vermouth*

2 dashes Regans' Orange Bitters No. 6

1 orange twist, studded with clove, as garnish

Stir with a classical colonial flair, strain into a chilled cocktail coupe whilst overthrowing the indigenous population and garnish with a clove-studded orange twist or an oppressive, corrupt political regime.

*Masala Sweet Vermouth: Take one 750-ml bottle of Indian merlot (Sula Satori in this case), fortify with 100 ml Honey Bee Indian brandy, and flavour with 1 gram of wormwood, 2 sticks of cinnamon, 5 cloves, 3 green cardamom pods, 1/2 barspoon of mace, a small pinch of saffron, 1 vanilla pod, dried sweet lime peel from 1 sweet lime. Let steep until the flavours blend, then strain and bottle.

265

Mumbai

30 ml (1 oz) wheat-based vodka

1 barspoon of Cardamom Dry Vermouth**

1 Kashmiri-chilli stuffed olive, as garnish

Shake over cracked ice for 10 seconds and double-strain into a chilled half-size cocktail glass. Garnish with a Kashmiri chilli-stuffed olive and an over-the-top Bollywood song and dance.

Cardamom Dry Vermouth: Infuse 1 bottle of Martini & Rossi Extra Dry vermouth with 8 crushed green cardamom pods for 5 days. Remove pods and rebottle.

gaz sez: *This is a drink that was tested by a mystery shopper as opposed to yours truly, and this guy, who travels to India regularly and is not a friend of Tim's, came back raving about the complexities of these side-by-siders, plus he loved having two mini drinks in front of him. I hope I get to Mumbai soon so I can try these cocktails. Failing that, though, perhaps I'll go to Bombay... .*

Isis

Adapted from a recipe by
**Grant Dingwall,
Corner Bar**,
Auckland, New Zealand.

"A martini-styled drink named after the Egyptian goddess who was worshipped as the ideal mother and wife, also the patron of nature and magic."
—Grant Dingwall.

45 ml (1.5 oz) Tanqueray No. TEN gin

15 ml (.5 oz) Chamomile and Jasmine Infused Dry Vermouth*

10 ml (.33 oz) Lillet Blanc

Stir over ice and strain into a chilled vintage cocktail coupe.

*Chamomile and Jasmine Infused Dry Vermouth: Pour one 750-ml bottle Dolin vermouth over 2 teaspoons chamomile tea leaves and 2 teaspoons jasmine tea leaves. Let stand for 1.5 to 2 hours, tasting while infusing to make sure the tea doesn't overpower the vermouth too much. Strain, bottle, and keep in the fridge for up to 2 months.

gaz sez: *Simple and beautiful. This one's a very subtle masterpiece, and its beauty lies in the fact that Grant didn't go overboard. I would have been so tempted to add a dash of orange bitters in this drink, but that would have thrown the whole thing out of whack. Well done, Grant.*

The Jefferson

Adapted from a recipe by
Jamie MacBain,
The Passenger,
Washington, D.C.

"While rather simple in ingredients and preparation, this drink is very layered and it keeps the drinker coming back for more."
—Jamie MacBain.

45 ml (1.5 oz) bourbon (preferably Bulleit)

22.5 ml (.75 oz) Carpano Antica

15 ml (.5 oz) crème de mûre

1 dash Fee Brothers Old Fashion bitters

1 lemon twist, as garnish

Stir over ice and strain into a chilled cocktail glass.
Squeeze the twist over the drink, then add as garnish.

gaz sez: *As Jamie notes, this is a simple formula, with the crème de mure being the most distinguishing factor and the Bulleit bourbon being a capable foil for the Carpano. Buffalo Trace works well in this one, too, and if you want to splash out, try the Jefferson with Michter's 25-year-old bourbon or rye—both pull the job off nicely.*

Jersey Girl

Adapted from a recipe by
Chad Doll,
Bryant's Cocktail Lounge,
Milwaukee, WI.

"I am a bartender, not a bar-chef, not a chef, not a mixologist, not a stir-mix-a lot ... I take all aspects of my job very
seriously and mixing or creating cocktails falls third in the
list of my job priorities. Right behind service and maintaining a comfortable environment for the patrons. I will not
laugh or make you feel like an idiot if you want a apple or
chocolate martini, flavored vodka and sprite, or a fist bump
delivered with your Jager Bomb."
—Chad Doll.

45 ml (1.5 oz) Luxardo Amaro Abano

22.5 ml (.75 oz) Ron Zacapa 23-year-old rum

1 orange twist, as garnish

Stir over ice and strain into a chilled champagne coupe.

Flame the twist over the drink, then add as garnish.

gaz sez: *I have a soft spot for Chad Doll. Here's
what I wrote about this drink in the San Francisco
Chronicle in 2010: "I'm featuring one of [Chad
Doll's] drinks here this week, and you'll notice that
it's about as simple as a recipe can be. Two ingredients and a garnish. Take this baby for a spin down
the coastline. She purrs like a pussy-cat, and packs
a punch like Muhammed Ali."*

Jive Turkey

Adapted from a recipe by
**Jessica Gonzalez,
Death & Co.**,
New York City, NY.

"I love to blend bourbon and rye. This is inspired by the
Brooklyn Cocktail as well."
—Jessica Gonzalez.

30 ml (1 oz) Wild Turkey rye whiskey

22.5 ml (.75 oz) Buffalo Trace bourbon

22.5 ml (.75 oz) Amaro CioCiaro

22.5 ml (.75 oz) dry vermouth

7.5 ml (.25 oz) St. Germain

1 dash Angostura bitters

Stir over ice and strain into a chilled cocktail glass.

gaz sez: *Jessica knows where my tastes lie, and the
Jive Turkey lives right on my street, just down the
road apiece from my Manhattan. The St. Germain
in this one adds a very interesting touch, and it's
because the recipe calls for such a small amount of
it that this drink is so well balanced.*

Kentucky Flyer

Adapted from a recipe by
Sierra Zimei,
Four Seasons,
San Francisco, CA.

"This is a play off of the Aviation but with good ol' 'merican
ingredients."
—Sierra Zimei.

60 ml (2 oz) rye whiskey

22.5 ml (.75 oz) Luxardo maraschino liqueur

15 ml (.5 oz) fresh lemon juice

1.5 fresh mint leaves

5 brandied cherries, as garnish

1 mint leaf, as garnish

Shake with ice and strain into a chilled cocktail glass.
Spear the cherries and mint on a pick and add as
garnish.

gaz sez: *Here's a very simple formula that trans-lates into a delightful quaff for a hot afternoon. I'm going to make this my new Kentucky Derby drink, I think.*

273

Laissez Les Bons Temps Rouler!

Adapted from a recipe by
**Bob Brunner,
Paragon Restaurant & Bar**,
Portland, OR.

"Let the good times roll! This cocktail was featured in the May 2010 issue of *Market Watch* magazine. A modern variation on the classic Sazerac cocktail, this one captivates!"
—Bob Brunner.

Marteau absinthe, as rinse

60 ml (2 oz) Russell's Reserve 6-year-old rye whiskey

15 ml (.5 oz) Cherry Heering

15 ml (.5 oz) Domain de Canton ginger liqueur

2 dashes Regans' Orange Bitters No. 6

1 orange twist, as garnish

Rinse a chilled cocktail glass with the absinthe; set aside. Stir the remaining ingredients over ice and strain into the glass. Add the garnish.

gaz sez: *Nice one, Bob—you consistently come up with some very solid drinks, and this one's no exception. It's the cherry/ginger thing that makes this one stand out so well.*

Lock and Key

Adapted from a recipe by
**Summer Voelker,
Salt of the Earth**,
Pittsburgh, PA.

"We could not get Strega in for a while and substituted .5 oz yellow Chartreuse. Still delicious!"
—Summer Voelker.

45 ml (1.5 oz) Buffalo Trace bourbon

15 ml (.5 oz) Strega

15 ml (.5 oz) Carpano Antica

15 ml (.5 oz) fresh lemon juice

3 drops Fee Brothers Whiskey Barrel Aged bitters, as garnish

1 mint leaf, as garnish

Shake all ingredients over ice and double-strain into a chilled coupe. Add the garnishes.

gaz sez: *I love the way in which the Buffalo Trace retains its integrity in this drink. It takes on the Strega and the Carpano, giving them room to dance in the ring, but it never lets either one of them get their licks in. Nice work if you can get it.*

275

Long Shot Kick de Bucket

Adapted from a recipe by
Ian Storror,
Future Inns,
Bristol, England.

"I wanted to come up with a long drink (as I don't normally), after trying a lot of long rum-based (rum's my favourite)
drinks I was left with a little something missing. I'd been
tending to drink my good rum with varying measures of
falernum and lime as in the West Indies, loving the simplic-

ity of flavour, but for a longer drink it needed something else. Experimented with various "Bucks" and decided to twist the original with a nice spiced sugar syrup with a little local pep (Somerset UK) and a sweet 'extra' to match the lime! It turned out to be the best long drink I've done and is so more-ish, it shouldn't date. Using the 50 ml of rum (Long Shot) and it being based on a Buck (Buck-et!) there was a natural choice for the name. The Pioneers song (late 1960s) of the same name (later covered by The Specials). It refers to a real legendary racehorse in Jamaica called "Long Shot" who was a long-lived but not very successful horse. Despite this many on the island loved it, backed it, and lost on it! On its 203rd race it came a cropper just as it was coming up the rail to win, a horse called Combat fell and brought down Long Shot! (check out the lyrics). Doh! Dead meat. When I did this for a comp', I used the in-house PA to play the track, starting to mix after the "Call to Post" trumpet blast. Mixing reggae style (soon come, steady as she goes), finishing and presenting at the end of the track to generous applause and whoops of great laughter. The drink went down well enough for Long Shot to win one for a change!"

—Ian Storror.

50 ml (1.65 oz) Havana Club Seleccion rum (or other decent aged rum)

25 ml (.83 oz) Somerset Cider brandy (or good calvados)

25 ml (.83 oz) fresh lime juice

30 ml (1 oz) Spiced Sugar Syrup*

1 barspoon maple syrup

Ginger ale

1 lime wedge, as garnish

1 star anise, as garnish

Shake over ice and strain over good-sized ice in a long glass (Poco Grande if available). Top with ginger ale and add the garnishes.

***Spiced Sugar Syrup**: Combine 720 ml (3 cups) water, 300 g (1.5 cups) brown sugar, 300 g (1.5 cups) demerara sugar, 1 cinnamon stick, 5 cloves, about 1 inch of peeled fresh ginger root, 3 cardomom pods, and 1 star anise in a saucepan. Warm gently until the sugar dissolves, 15 minutes tops. Cool, strain the spices, and bottle.

gaz sez: *Phew! Ian can be pretty longwinded, huh? Great drink, though. I used Appleton VX rum and Laird's Bottled-in-Bond applejack. It worked very well, indeed. It's the spice syrup that makes this baby stand out.*

Malecon

Adapted from a recipe by
Erik Lorincz,
The American Bar at the Savoy Hotel,
London, UK.

"I have read that the essence of what it means to be Cuban is to accept the inevitabilities of human existence, that we are born and must die, and to make the very best of the life in-between and have as good a time as possible. With this admirable attitude in mind, I wanted to create a drink that could be enjoyed at any time of day or night, and that would be at home in the most elegant London cocktail bar and equally at the Malecon in Havana with music, laughter, and tobacco smoke in the air. My drink offers the freshness of lime, the rich fruit and nuts of aged port and sherry, and bitter counterpoint of the Peychaud's bitters, all wrapped up in the smooth warmth of Bacardi rum. Enjoy it and enjoy life!"

—Erik Lorincz.

50 ml (1.65 oz) Bacardi Superior rum

15 ml (.5 oz) Smith Woodhouse 10 year old tawny port

10 ml (.33 oz) Don José Oloroso sherry

30 ml (1 oz) fresh lime juice

2 barspoons sugar

3 dashes Peychaud's bitters

1 crystal-clear ice cube, as garnish

Shake over large ice cubes and fine-strain into a chilled crystal coupette. Add the garnish.

gaz sez: *I wrote about this one for the San Francisco Chronicle (December 19, 2010). Here's an excerpt: "Malecon is a fabulous drink, and if you try it, you'll know why the Savoy sought him out for its new landmark bar. If you can't find the specific ingredients he calls for, don't let that stop you. Use a decent port, a good oloroso sherry and a white rum of your choice. Then drink to the inevitabilities of human existence. You won't get out of here alive, you know."*

Marmalade Sour

Adapted from a recipe by
**Casey Robison,
Barrio**,
Seattle, WA.

1 egg white

2 barspoons orange marmalade

60 ml (2 oz) Corralejo blanco tequila

30 ml (1 oz) fresh lemon juice

3 dashes Scrappy's Lavender bitters

1 orange twist, as garnish

Dry-shake, then add ice. Shake and double-strain into
a chilled coupe. Flame the orange twist over the drink,
then add as garnish.

gaz sez: *If you haven't tried Scrappy's Lavender bitters (www.scrappysbitters.com), then this is a drink that will serve you well if you make it in order to see what they can bring to a cocktail. The interplay between the marmalade and the bitters is just incredible in the Marmalade Sour, and the tequila serves as a gracious host for the match.*

Martilla

Adapted from a recipe by
**Bas Verhoeven,
Door 74**,
Amsterdam, Netherlands.

"This real smooth drink is my signature drink and one of the best-selling cocktails at Door 74 in Amsterdam. You will take journey and taste every flavor step-by-step, and the tequila is the last taste you would expect to find in this sublime drink."
—Bas Verhoeven.

1 barspoon lemon zest

45 ml (1.5 oz) Don Julio añejo tequila

3 barspoons Luxardo maraschino liqueur

30 ml (1 oz) Noilly Prat dry vermouth

1 lemon twist, as garnish

Put the lemon zest in a mixing glass and fill it with cubed ice. Add the remaining ingredients and stir for 10 seconds depending on the ice. Double-strain into a chilled cocktail glass and add the garnish.

gaz sez: *Keep it simple and the day will be yours. I've no doubt that this baby sells like wildfire at Door 74. It's a session cocktail. One's too many and three is not enough.*

Marquee

Adapted from a recipe by
Cris Dehlavi,
M Restaurant and Bar,
Columbus, OH.

"My inspiration for the Marquee came right after I tasted Cointreau Noir—such a lovely spirit—and I knew I wanted to make something exceptional with it. The combination of its sweetness with the tart fresh blood orange and the Angostura bitters makes for a really well balanced cocktail. The restaurant I work at is simply called "M"—hence the design in the egg white."
—Cris Dehlavi.

30 ml (1 oz) Cointreau Noir

30 ml (1 oz) Belvedere Cytrus vodka

15 ml (.5 oz) fresh lemon juice

15 ml (.5 oz) fresh blood orange juice

7.5 ml (.25 oz) agave nectar

1 egg white

Angostura bitters, as garnish

Dry-shake, then add ice. Hard-shake and strain into a chilled cocktail glass. Using a stencil with "M" logo, lightly spray Angostura bitters on to top of cocktail.

gaz sez: *I LOVE Belvedere Cytrus, and she plays her role nicely in Marquee. No, I didn't get myself a stencil to test this one, but I did add the bitters as an aromatic garnish, just like on top of a Pisco Sour. Works well.*

Martini Zen

Adapted from a recipe by
Matt Peckham,
Liquidchefs Cocktail Lounge,
Johannesburg, South Africa.

"We have a couple of bars, including MiBar, that were sponsored by Martini. This is one of the signature cocktails and is very popular. The Mi stands for 'meaningful interaction,' and the bars are designed with multimedia platforms. It is where online social networks meet and interact in the real world."
—Matt Peckham.

8 to 12 mint leaves

20 ml (.66 oz) runny honey

12.5 ml (.42 oz) fresh lemon juice

25 ml Martini & Rossi Bianco vermouth

25 ml (.83 oz) Grey Goose vodka

25 ml (.83 oz) iced brewed Lipton green tea

Bianco Mint Foam*, as garnish

1 mint sprig, as garnish

Muddle the mint and honey in a mixing glass. Add ice and the remaining ingredients. Shake hard and double-strain into a chilled cocktail glass. Top with foam and add the garnish.

***Bianco Mint Foam**: Muddle 20 to 24 mint leaves with 25 ml (.83 oz) Monin Miel syrup in the mixing glass of a Boston shaker. Add 1 egg white, 50 ml (1.65 oz) Martini & Rossi Bianco vermouth and 25 ml (.83 oz) fresh lemon juice. Shake hard and fine-strain into a whipped cream canister. Charge with 2 nitrogen cartridges.

285

gaz sez: *Jeez this drink was a pain in the ass to make, but it was bloody delightful to sip. I think that a trip to South Africa is in order... .*

My Way Manhattan

Adapted from a recipe by
Daniel-Grigore Mostenaru,
Radisson Hotel,
Bucharest, Romania.

The following text originally appeared in *The San Francisco Chronicle*.

It took Daniel-Grigore Mostenaru, a bartender from Bucharest, to really nail a drink called the My Way Manhattan, so I sort of think of him as being the Sid Vicious of classic cocktails. I do hope that he approves.

It took me a little while to translate the recipe that Mostenaru sent to me, but that had nothing to do with English not being his native tongue. It was his units of measurement that made me ponder a little.

He didn't use fluid ounces, of course. We're the last nation on the face of the earth to use that system, I think. Are you listening, Mister President? But he didn't use the metric system, either. Instead, Mostenaru presented his ingredients in terms of time.

He called for "60 minutes of Four Roses bourbon, 30 minutes of Dubonnet Rouge, 1 second of orange curaçao, 1 second of Branca Menta." And he went on to instruct, "first mist your mixing glass with seconds, then add the minutes, the ice, and stir for about 23 to 24 seconds." Daniel-Grigore Mostenaru has a way with words, I believe.

I'll let this Bucharest bartender have the last word on this drink, I think. He described it as a "beautiful variation of a never-die cocktail with subtle flavours of bitters, fruit, and

287

spices. It's an underground drink for people whom enjoy a nice measure of bourbon." Well said, Daniel-Grigore Mostenaru. Well said.

7.5 ml (.25 oz) orange curaçao

7.5 ml (.25 oz) Branca Menta

60 ml (2 oz) Four Roses bourbon

30 ml (1 oz) Dubonnet Rouge

1 lemon twist, as garnish

Pour the curaçao and the Branca Menta into an empty mixing glass, and swirl the liquids around so as to coat the interior of the glass. Add ice and the remaining ingredients. Stir well and strain into a chilled champagne coupe. Add the garnish.

Napoleon's Itch

Adapted from a recipe by
Toby McMillen,
Mistral Restaurant & Bar,
Redwood City, CA.

"I based this upon the classic Corpse Reviver #2."
—Toby McMillen.

30 ml (1 oz) Mandarine Napoléon

22.5 ml (.75 oz) Leopold's Small Batch gin

22.5 ml (.75 oz) Dolin Blanc vermouth

22.5 ml (.75 oz) fresh lemon juice

3 to 4 drops Regans' Orange Bitters No. 6

1 Luxardo maraschino cherry, as garnish

Shake over ice and double-strain into chilled small
cocktail glass. Add the garnish.

gaz sez: *This is an interesting take on the CR2. I couldn't get my hands on a bottle of Leopold's so I made this one with Beefeater, Tanqueray, and Plymouth. They all worked well, and they all played nice with the Mandarine Napoléon. Who'd have thunk it? I should also mention that Leopold's gin was named as Best American Gin, 2009, by the Wall Street Journal, so I'll be seeking it out real soon.*

Negroni d'Or

Adapted from a recipe by
**Brian MacGregor,
Locanda**,
San Francisco, CA.

"Gaz, I recall you loving this drink at the G'vine summer party/ball, also I think that night it took second to Stephen Hinz cocktail, although I did not do so hot in the rest of the competition."
—Brian MacGregor.

45 ml (1.5 oz) G'vine Nouasion gin

15 ml (.5 oz) Dolin Blanc vermouth

15 ml (.5 oz) Grand Classico bitter*

Stir over ice and strain into a chilled sherry glass.

***Gran Classico Bitter** is based on the original "Bitter of Turin" recipe dating from the 1860's. This classic aperitif is an infusion of numerous herbs and roots including bitter orange peel, wormwood, gentian, rhubarb, and other aromatic plants. Gran Classico Bitter's color is a natural result of the herbs and plants infused into pure grain spirit produced to the highest Swiss standards and is not artificially colored in any way.
(http://www.granclassico.com/)

gaz sez: *Brian made this for the finals of the G'Vine Best Gin Bartender Competition in Paris, June, 2010 where I was a judge alongside the intrepid Phillip Duff and Jean-Sebastian Robriquet, head honcho at G'Vine, and a guy who I really love and admire—he's a liquor producer with the soul of a bartender. I think I knocked back about five of these babies that night. Need I say more?*

The Nervous Light of Sunday

Adapted from a recipe by
**Michael Yusko,
CURE**,
New Orleans, LA.

"The name of the cocktail comes from the title of a chapter in Fred Exley's 1968 novel *A Fan's Notes,* about an obsessive, alcoholic New York Giants fan. Although the cocktail is delicious and refreshing any time of year, I always think it to be best enjoyed on the Sunday mornings leading up to the big game."
—Michael Yusko.

60 ml (2 oz) gin (Tanqueray is used at Cure; Beefeater
and Plymouth also work well)

30 ml (1 oz) fresh lemon juice

22.5 ml (.75 oz) Luxardo bitters

15 ml (.5 oz) simple syrup (1:1)

14 drops Fee Brothers Old Fashion bitters

14 drops Fee Brothers Grapefruit bitters

1 grapefruit twist, as garnish

Shake all ingredients over ice and strain over ice into a
rocks glass.

gaz sez: *Here's another oddity that works well despite itself. The three different styles of bitters, with Luxardo up front, make The Nervous Light Of Sunday a very complex cocktail, and it's a high-octane baby, too. Just like I like 'em!*

New Amsterdam

Adapted from a recipe by
Mathew Giblin,
42 at the Ritz-Carlton,
White Plains, NY.

90 ml (3 oz) Bols Genever

30 ml (1 oz) Noilly Prat sweet vermouth

1 dash Fee Brothers Whiskey Barrel Aged bitters

1 dash Regans' Orange Bitters No. 6

1 Luxardo maraschino cherry, as garnish

Stir over ice and strain into a chilled cocktail glass. Add
the garnish.

gaz sez: *Nice and simple and absolutely fabulous.*
My kinda drink.

North Garden

Adapted from a recipe by
**Jason Littrell,
Dram**
and
Death & Co.,
New York City, NY.

"This is basically an applejack Old-Fashioned. It's got enough light peat that it is there, but doesn't take over the apples. The wood from the bourbon gives it class, but the applejack is the real star of the show. Demerara lends texture and binds the flavors, while the Angostura pulls the whole thing together."
—Jason Littrell.

1 dash Angostura bitters

1 teaspoon demerara sugar syrup (2:1)

7.5 ml (.25 oz) Laphroaig 10 Year Old scotch whisky

22.5 ml (.75 oz) Buffalo Trace bourbon

45 ml (1.5 oz) Laird's 100 Proof apple brandy

Stir over ice and strain into a chilled rocks glass. Add a big ice cube.

gaz sez: *This one's right up my alley. I didn't even go up on the bitters when I made it, cos I kinda sorta knew that the fairy-dust in the gem was going to be the Laphroaig. You didn't let me down, Jason.*

293

Oceana

Adapted from a recipe by
**Ektoras Binikos,
Oceana**,
New York City, NY.

1 shiso leaf

1 small piece Serrano pepper (very small, be careful with the heat)

30 ml (1 oz) Shiso Syrup*

45 ml (1.5 oz) Fjallagros-Infused Vodka**

15 ml (.5 oz) Cointreau

15 ml (.5 oz) pasteurized egg whites

45 ml (1.5 oz) yuzu juice

15 ml (.5 oz) fresh lime juice

Seaweed, as garnish

Muddle the shiso leaf, pepper, and syrup in a mixing glass. Add ice and the remaining ingredients. Shake well and strain into a chilled coupe. Add the garnish.

***Shiso Syrup**: Combine 150 g (5 oz) shiso leaves, 1500 g (7.5 cups) sugar, 1.5L (6.25 cups) water, and 3/4 tablespoon salt in a saucepan. Bring to a boil, then remove from heat and let cool to room temperature. Refrigerate, then strain the next day. This will keep for a month.

****Fjallagros-Infused Vodka**: Fjalla-gros is a lichen that grows in Iceland where it's usually used to make a milky soup called **Fjallagrasam-jólk.** If you cannot find it, use dried kelp. Combine 25 g (1 oz) fjallagros with one 750-ml bottle of vodka in a glass jar. Refrigerate for 2 weeks, then strain, bottle, and store in the refrigerator.

gaz sez: *Thank God I didn't have to make this one up to test it—a trip to Oceana sampling this, and about five more fabulous cocktails, was all it took to discover that this really is one mother of a drink. I can't even describe this sucker, but it's sure as hell unusual, and complex. Ektoras is one cool dude.*

Oz

Adapted from a recipe by
**Lynn House,
Blackbird**,
Chicago, IL.

"Oz is the name of the jazz club where Pierre Ferrand first made its American debut. Ironically I lived just a few blocks away and was a frequent patron. Master Distiller Alexandre Gabriel and I bonded over this discovery. I promised that my next cognac cocktail would feature the Ambre and be called Oz."
—Lynn House.

45 ml (1.5 oz) Pierre Ferrand Ambre cognac

45 ml (1.5 oz) plum wine

15 ml (.5 oz) fresh lemon juice

15 ml (.5 oz) Apple Cider Gastrique*

30 ml (1 oz) Gruet Blanc de Noirs

1 lemon twist, as garnish

Shake the cognac, wine, lemon juice, and Gastrique over ice until well chilled. "Roll" on the Gruet (pour it into the glass and gently roll, or you can stir). Strain into a chilled coupe and add the garnish.

***Apple Cider Gastrique**: Combine 720 ml (3 cups) apple cider vinegar and 1,400 g (7 cups) sugar in a saucepan and simmer for 1 hour. Cool and strain into bottles.

gaz sez: *Jeez-Louise, there's a helluva lot of talent in this drink. The balance is perfect, the combination of ingredients shows true genius, and the use of Pierre Ferrand Ambre shows a confidence that's hard to come by. Lynn House rocks.*

Parisian Barmaid

Adapted from a recipe for Valentine's Day by
**Erick Castro,
The Rickhouse**,
San Francisco, CA.

"Tread lightly, for this busty treasure is every bit as alluring and rambunctious as her name suggests. Flirtatious yet delightful, this playful beverage is ideal for anyone who does not believe that style and substance should remain mutually exclusive."
—Rickhouse Cocktail Menu, February, 2010.

60 ml (2 oz) Martell VS cognac

15 ml (.5 oz) Rothman & Winter apricot liqueur

22.5 ml (.75 oz) fresh lemon juice

15 ml (.5 oz) simple syrup

2 dashes Angostura bitters

1 Duke's Lemon,* as garnish

Shake over ice and strain into a large chilled coupe. Add the garnish.

*A very large lemon twist.

gaz sez: *This one's another nice and simple drink that just happens to work very well indeed, and makes good use of the Martell cognac, a fine brand if ever there was one. I also like the way that the Angostura plays with the apricot liqueur in the Parisian Barmaid. Rothman & Winter is such a distinguished brand. We owe much to Eric Seed in the USA for bringing their products, and many other great brands, to our shores.*

Parisienne Daisy

Adapted from a recipe by
**Francesco Cione,
Caffè Baglioni at Carlton Hotel**,
Milan, Italy.

"Made for the cocktail menu of the Carlton Hotel Baglioni in Milan, this became pretty famous after an article appeared on the local Milan section of the *Corriere della Sera*."
—Francesco Cione.

4 fresh pineapple chunks

2 to 3 drops The Bitter Truth Jerry Thomas' Own Decanter bitters

45 ml (1.5 oz) Hendrick's gin

15 ml (.5 oz) St. Germain

1o ml (.33 oz) La Fée Absinthe Parisienne (68% abv)

15 ml (.5 oz) fresh lemon juice (preferably from Amalfi lemons)

2 thin cucumber slices, as garnish

2 raspberries, as garnish

1 mint sprig, as garnish

Muddle the pineapple and bitters in a mixing glass. Add ice and the remaining ingredients. Shake well and double-strain into a chilled goblet with a few ice cubes. Add the garnishes.

gaz sez: *I adore The Bitter Truth's Jerry Thomas' Own Decanter bitters, and I sometimes use them in my Manhattans instead of Angostura, so when I saw this recipe I had a feeling that I was going to love this drink. There's nothing in there not to love, right? As usual, though, it's important to point out that the absinthe can take over almost any drink if not used judiciously, so be careful out there.*

Pernelle

Adapted from a recipe by
Colin Asare-Appiah,
New York City, NY.

"Pernelle was the wife of Hermes the Alchemist. Behind every great man is a great woman, and this cocktail is a nod to them."
—Colin Asare-Appiah.

1 rosemary sprig

1 barspoon agave syrup

60 ml (2 oz) U'Luvka vodka

15 ml (.5 oz) pear eau de vie or poire William

30 ml (1 oz) St. Germain

30 ml (1 oz) fresh lemon juice

Club soda

1 rosemary sprig, as garnish

1 lemon twist, as garnish

Muddle the rosemary and syrup in a mixing glass. Add the remaining ingredients except soda. Shake without ice and strain into a highball glass filled with crushed ice. Add the soda and garnishes.

gaz sez: *I wonder why Colin chose U'Luvka vodka for this drink? For full disclosure's sake I should let everyone know that Colin is an ambassador for U'Luvka, and I should also let everyone know that Pernelle is a damned fine drink. To borrow Audrey Saunders' analogy, Colin has used the vodka like a blank canvas, and oh what a pretty picture he's painted upon it. The play twixt the rosemary and the St. Germain is a joy to behold.*

299

Point of View

Adapted from a recipe by
**René Förster,
Twist Bar**,
Dresden, Germany.

40 ml (1.33 oz) Zacapa 23-year-old rum

20 ml (.66 oz) cream sherry

20 ml (.66 oz) yellow Chartreuse

2 dashes The Bitter Truth Chocolate bitters

1 dash The Bitter Truth Orange bitters

1 orange twist, as garnish

1 maraschino cherry, as garnish

Stir over ice and strain in a chilled cocktail glass. Add
the garnishes.

gaz sez: *This is a fabulously orchestrated cocktail
with the Zacapa and the sherry taking center stage,
the Chartreuse chiming in as second female lead,
and the bitters quietly playing the xylophone in the
background. Nicely done, René.*

Pomp and Glory

Adapted from a recipe by
Hayden Lambert,
formerly at
The Merchant Hotel,
Belfast, Northern Ireland.

"The P & G is based on the Bamboo Cocktail, which was created sometime around the 1890s by Louis Eppinger at the Grand Hotel in Yokohama, Japan."

—Hayden Lambert.

30 ml (1 oz) fino sherry

20 ml (.66 oz) St. Germain

5 ml (.17 oz) fresh lemon juice

2 dashes orange bitters

1 drop Angostura bitters

1 lemon twist, as garnish

Stir over ice and strain into a small cordial glass ... the more audacious the better. Add the garnish.

gaz sez: *Hmmm ... I know Hayden Lambert. Met him when he was working at the Merchant Hotel in Belfast and Wondrich and I were there to do a dog-and-pony show in 2008. I was the warm-up act for Dave. Jeez, my career's just going straight down the drain.... . Anyway, Haydes, as he likes to call himself, is an affable chappie, and this drink works very well indeed, though it's a far cry from the Bamboo, a drink that calls for dry sherry, dry vermouth, and both orange and Angostura bitters. There's no citrus in a Bamboo. Mind you, I can see how the lemon juice got in there. He substituted St. Germain for the vermouth, and he needed to balance out the sweetness with a little sour. Works well, Haydes.*

Pooja du Pina

Adapted from a recipe by
**Oron Lerner,
Mapal**,
Haifa, Israel.

4 fresh pineapple cubes, about 1 cm (.5 in)

1 barspoon dried lavender flowers

30 ml (1 oz) Lemon Hart 151 Demerara rum (or other
overproof rum)

30 ml (1 oz) Appleton Estate 12 Year Old rum (or other
aged Jamaican rum)

30 ml (1 oz) Havana Club Añejo 3 Años rum (or other
Cuban or Puerto Rican rum)

30 ml (1 oz) fresh lemon juice

30 ml (1 oz) agave syrup

1 dash Angostura bitters

Pineapple leaves, as garnish

Fresh lavender, as garnish

Muddle the pineapple and lavender in a mixing glass.
Add ice and the remaining ingredients. Shake very very
hard and strain into a tiki glass. Garnish extensively with
pineapple leaves and fresh lavender.

gaz sez: *How cool is this drink, huh? The lavender
and the pineapple are a fabulous match for one another, and the overproof rum gives this baby a kick
that suits my palate well. I used Bacardi 8 instead
of the Havana Club, and the drink came together
very nicely indeed.*

Puesta del Sol

Adapted from a recipe by
**Rick Tose,
The Classroom**,
Manchester, England.

"I was doing a few guest shifts while home on holiday and was trying out a recipe to submit in a local Jameson's cocktail comp the bar was about to hold. It's a summer sipper, playing on the earthy, yet vanilla and sherry characteristics of the whiskey, by complementing them with heather and spice which match perfectly with stone fruit. The drink is then lifted with citrus and a dash of bitters rounds it off nicely, lifting noticeable hints of the Drambuie through. The customer said she could sit and drink these all evening by the water as the sun went down, hence the name Puesta del Sol (sunset)."
—Rick Tose.

After telling Rick that his drink had been chosen for inclusion here, he wrote, "One thing I forgot to tell you about (totally not on purpose), was that the name of the drink was originally called "Gorgeous Gus" after the nickname given to one of the coopers (Willie McCann) at the Jameson's Distillery by John Jameson. It was cheeky and reflected the drink and the style of drink, whilst giving a nod to the clientele of whom the soft introduction to whiskey would appeal! The name change was due to the fact that anyone who geeked-up for a Jameson's Comp could have called their drink the Gorgeous Gus and potentially there could be a few of them! I think Puesta del Sol fits it nicely, but as it is your publication you are more than welcome to use the original-name story or give a nod to it in

305

the descriptions!" Thanks, Rick. You're one strange dude, but the Manchester thing explains much.

30 ml (1 oz) Jameson's Irish whiskey

20 ml (.66 oz) Bols apricot brandy

10 ml (.33 oz) Drambuie

20 ml (.66 oz) fresh lemon juice

10 to 15 ml (.33 to .5 oz) simple syrup, or to taste

1 hefty dash Angostura bitters

1 dried apricot, as garnish

1 mint sprig, as garnish

1 lemon twist, as garnish

Combine all the ingredients in a mixing glass, add ice, and shake it like it owes you money. Strain over crushed ice in a chilled short glass, crown with crushed ice, and add the garnishes.

gaz sez: *I've seen people in Manchester get the hell beaten out of them for coming out with flowery prose such as Rick's description of this drink, but I must say that he just about nails it, and I love the way the apricot brandy plays pretty with the Drambuie in this one. Nicely done, Rick.*

Punch de Chevalier

Adapted from a recipe by
Merlin Jerebine, 1806,
Melbourne, Australia.

"I came up with this drink when playing around with the punch family. I like the punchy herbal notes of this drink. I entered The Suntory Cup, a cocktail comp in Australia, and won with this drink."
—Merlin Jerebine.

25 ml (.83 oz) Remy Martin VSOP cognac

20 ml (.66 oz) green Chartreuse

15 ml (.5 oz) Gabriel Boudier crème de pêche

30 ml (1 oz) fresh lemon juice

10 ml (.33 oz) sugar syrup

2 lemon wedges, as garnish

Shake over ice and strain into a highball glass over fresh ice. Add the garnish.

gaz sez: *It's no wonder that this one took the cake at the competition—it's a damned masterpiece! Why? Because the Chartreuse and the crème de pêche* get down to some very serious sex in this glass, and the result is one very sophisticated child who stands up to be counted. The Remy provides the venue, and the lemon juice and simple syrup add dimension. Fabulous. Just fabulous.*

* I used Massenez crème de pêche cos Painter's didn't have Boudier.

307

Queen Eleanor

Adapted from a recipe by
Brandon Josie,
15 Romolo,
San Francisco, CA.

"From Queen Consort in France to Queen of England, Eleanor of Aquitaine was worth talking about. So take a trip from France to England with this twist on a gin martini.... It'll be worth talking about."
—Brandon Josie.

45 ml (1.5 oz) gin

15 ml (.5 oz) dry vermouth

15 ml (.5 oz) crème de pêche

1 dash The Bitter Truth Original Celery bitters

1 lemon twist, as garnish

Stir over ice and strain into a chilled cocktail glass. Add the garnish.

gaz sez: *Peach and celery can't possible work well together, right? Wrong. This cocktail's a winner all the way.*

Que Rico!

Adapted from a recipe by
**Merlin Griffiths,
Priory Tavern**,
London, UK.

"Created for Bombay Sapphire food pairing events when challenged by a chef to use gin in a digestif cocktail rather than an aperitif. The name came from David Cordoba, Global Ambassador for Bacardi Rums, who on tasting it exclaimed, '*que rico!*' (which translates literally to 'how rich!')."
—Merlin Griffiths.

40 ml (1.33 oz) Bombay Sapphire gin

40 ml (1.33 oz) Romate Cardenal Cisneros Pedro
Ximénez sherry

10 ml (.33 oz) crème d'abricot (Merlet brand is good)

1 drop Angostura orange bitters

1 large orange twist, as garnish

Combine all the ingredients in a mixing glass with plenty
of ice. Stir gently until cold and syrup-like. Strain into a
chilled ISO tasting glass*, a Glencairn glass, or a chilled
brandy balloon. Squeeze the twist over the cocktail,
expressing the oils before using the twist as a garnish.
Sip and savour.

*International Standards Organisation glass: http://
www.winebox.co.uk/ISO-Wine-Tasting-Glass

gaz sez: *I don't care what kind of glass you serve this one in, don't miss this drink. Gin and PX work really well together, and the layers and layers of flavors in the Que Rico! are just amazing. I should also note that Merlin's choice of Angostura orange bitters is a wise one in this case—they add a touch of bitterness that most other brands, my own included, don't carry, and it provides a good foil for the PX. And yes, I'm quite aware that Merlin does a bit of shilling for Bombay Sapphire, but that can't stop me from recognizing a damned good drink.*

The Red Violin

Adapted from a recipe by
Mike Henderson,
Colt & Gray,
Denver, CO.

30 ml (1 oz) Plymouth gin

15 ml (.5 oz) Crème Yvette

15 ml (.5 oz) simple syrup

7.5 ml (.25 oz) fresh lemon juice

2 dashes Peychaud's bitters

Champagne or prosecco

1 lemon twist, as garnish

Shake all ingredients except champagne vigorously
over ice for 10 seconds and double-strain into a chilled
champagne flute. Top with champagne and add the
garnish.

gaz sez: *Get ready for this drink to blow your mind. Why? It's the marriage of the Crème Yvette and the Peychaud's bitters that creates such a fabulous flowery-anise explosion on the palate, and the Plymouth is the perfect magic carpet to carry these guys to Nirvana.*

Remnants of Summer

Adapted from a recipe by
**Matt Seiter,
Sanctuaria**,
Saint Louis, MO.

"Originally this was made with leftover cucumber-infused
tequila from our summer menu, hence the name of this
cocktail. We made that by slicing one English cucumber per
bottle of tequila (we used Espalon silver) and letting it sit
for three days. I recommend using the infused tequila, but
the muddled version works just as well."

—Matt Seiter.

2 cucumber slices (1/4 inch thick), quartered

22.5 ml (.75 oz) fresh lime juice

15 ml (.5 oz) maraschino liqueur

45 ml (1.5 oz) tequila

10 ml (.33 oz) Fernet Branca

30 ml (1 oz) Cava

1 paper-thin cucumber slice, as garnish

Muddle the cucumber, lime, and liqueur in a mixing glass. Add ice and the remaining ingredients. Rock the drink 18 times and fine-strain into a chilled coupe. Float the garnish on top.

gaz sez: *I'm not a big fan of cucumber, but I love this drink. The flavors are all over the place. The maraschino seems to be duking it out with the Fernet whilst the lime juice is playing second to both and neither of them at the same time. Ted Kilgore's influence is obvious here, but Matt has brought his own asana into play within this drink, too.*

313

Ruby Can't Fail

Adapted from a recipe by
**Julian de Feral,
Lutyens**,
London, UK.

"Having worked behind the stick for over ten years, and having created mixed drinks for over five, I have never sent you a recipe despite being a 'Joy … ' fan. To make up for this misdemeanour, here are twenty. That should keep you busy … That's all for now until, perhaps, 2020. Merry Christmas, bottoms up, and enjoy!"
—Julian de Feral.

35 ml (1.17 oz) gin

15 ml (.5 oz) ruby port

15 ml (.5 oz) fresh lemon juice

10 ml (.33 oz) fino sherry

10 ml (.33 oz) simple syrup

1 dash Regans' Orange Bitters No. 6

1 lemon twist

1 pink grapefruit twist

Shake over ice and strain into a chilled fancy wine glass.
Squeeze the twists over the drink, then discard.

gaz sez: *Julian says that he created this one when he worked at Milk & Honey in London, and I've got to say that I was taken aback to see gin marrying port in a glass. It was a concept I'd never considered. Or at least I thought I'd never considered it. When I wrote to him about this concept Julian promptly reminded me that at the last night of* *the Diageo Reserve World Class Finals in Athens, 2010, I was making pink drinks with T10 and port when I sneaked behind the bar to work alongside Angus Winchester for half an hour or so. "And that was my port," Julian told me. Busted again. I really like Julian's style when it comes to drink creation, and this one shows him off nicely, I think.*

Rum 'n' Raisin

Adapted from a recipe by
**Paul Lambert,
SABA**,
Dublin, Ireland.

"The wonderful rich fruit notes in the sherry complement the dried fruit notes in the rum. The sherry influence in the whisky also contributes to the aroma. A simple twist on the Daiquirí and a tribute to the favourite ice cream of the 1980s … enjoy!"

—Paul Lambert.

15ml (.5 oz) fresh lime juice

2 barspoons caster sugar (sold as superfine sugar in the land of ounces)

50ml (1.65 oz) Bacardi Superior rum

10 ml (.33 oz) Pedro Ximenez sherry

Auchentoshan Three Wood scotch whisky, in a mister

3 raisins, as garnish

Squeeze the lime juice into a shaker, then add the sugar and stir. Add the rum and sherry. Add ice and shake hard. Double-strain into a chilled cocktail glass. Spray with the scotch three times, then add the garnish.

gaz sez: *The rum and sherry work well in this drink, but it's the misting of the Auchentoshan that brings glory to this drink. That's a very nice move, indeed.*

St. Clement's Stone Sour

Adapted from a recipe by
Alex Orwin,
The Rushmore Group
(formally The Match Bar Group),
London, UK.

"Developed in October 2010 for The Starland Social Club, the newest member's space in The Rushmore Group. The menu here is handwritten weekly, giving the Head Bartender the scope to offer drinks that are seasonal and that really demonstrate his craft. I think this drink does both. Clementines are bang in season now and their bright floral flavours are clean and uplifting as the dark evenings draw in. Clove and other dark spice notes in the bitters work effortlessly with the clementine and are evocative of the incoming festive season. The delicate botanicals in Beefeater 24 bring all these elements together in what is ultimately a drink that is tasty, refreshing and morish, as all great drinks should be!"
—Alex Orwin.

40 ml (1.33 oz) Beefeater 24 gin

5 ml (.17 oz) Luxardo maraschino liqueur

30 ml (1 oz) fresh clementine juice

20 ml (.66 oz) fresh lemon juice

15 ml (.5 oz) simple syrup (1:1)

20 ml (.66 oz) egg white

1 dash Angostura bitters

Dry-shake, then add ice. Hard-shake and strain into a frozen coupette. There is no extra garnish; the foam IS the garnish!

gaz sez: *Stone sours usually contain orange juice as well as lemon or lime juice, and the clementine juice used here adds a distinctly lighter note than regular orange juice would normally yield. This is just one of the reasons that this drink caught my eye. Alex describes this drink to a T in the introduction, and what I like best about this one is the fact that the Beefeater 24 shines right through the drink. That, I think, is the true beauty of it. The botanicals in B 24 are, indeed, delicate, but they are all evident in the St. Clement's Stone Sour, and that hint of maraschino (I used Luxardo when I tested the recipe) dances nicely in the back of the throat making this a pretty complex potion, indeed. Nicely done, Alex.*

Sapphire Starburst

Adapted from a recipe by
**Anthony DeSerio,
Aspen Restaurant**,
Old Saybrook, CT.

"Classic meets contemporary. This is a smooth and silky aperitif, based on some of the most known gin cocktails. It is part Negroni, part Sour, part Daisy, with a little bit of a Flip (sans egg yolk). Combined with a modern take using new products, blended with an adapted simple syrup to create a molecular foam garnish that brings you back for that extra sip. The herbal notes of the Earl Grey and ginger of the foam help to marry the Earl Grey and citrus of the cocktail. Either of which equally are enhanced by or bring out the botanicals that make Bombay Sapphire."
—Anthony DeSerio.

45 ml (1.5 oz) Bombay Sapphire gin

22.5 ml (.75 oz) Aperol

30 ml (1 oz) Earl Grey Simple Syrup*

37.5 ml (1.25 oz) RIPE Fresh/Agave sour mix (or 30 ml [1 oz] fresh lemon juice and 7.5 ml [.25 oz] agave nectar)

3 dashes Regans' Orange Bitters No. 6

Earl Grey Ginger Foam**, as garnish

1 orange twist, as garnish

Shake over ice and strain into a chilled cocktail glass.
Add the garnishes.

***Earl Grey Simple Syrup**: Combine 200 g (1 cup) sugar, 240 ml (1 cup) boiling water and 3 Earl Grey tea bags. Stir until the sugar dissolves, then steep a few minutes longer. Remove the tea bags, bottle, and store in the refrigerator._

**Earl Grey Ginger Foam: Whisk 1 pasteurized egg white in a small bowl until foamy. Slowly pour in 45 ml (1.5 oz) Domain de Canton ginger liqueur and 30 ml (1 oz) Earl Grey Simple Syrup while whisking continuously and aggressively into frothy strong foam.

gaz sez: *This was another pain-in-the-ass drink to put together, but I've a lot of time for Anthony—he's the real deal—so put it together I did, and the reward was heavenly. Keep it up, Anthony.*

Scot Salute

Adapted from a recipe by
**Jim Meehan,
PDT**,
New York City, NY.

In celebration of the tenth anniversary of Compass Box, the revolutionary scotch whisky company founded by pioneering American blender John Glaser, Jim blended a couple of his favorite marks into a variation upon the Prince Edward Cocktail.

45 ml (1.5 oz) Cocchi Americano

30 ml (1 oz) Compass Box Orangerie scotch whisky

30 ml (1 oz) Compass Box Peat Monster Reserve
scotch whisky

1 dash Regans' Orange Bitters No. 6

1 dash Angostura bitters

1 lemon twist, as garnish

Stir over ice and strain into a chilled coupe. Add the
garnish.

gaz sez: *Jeez, this is one helluva complex drink. The bitters get a little lost here, I think, but the play between the Cocchi Americano, the Orangerie, and the Peat Monster (one of my fave scotches), is like a rough and tumble in the schoolyard where everyone comes out smiling. This one's pretty fabulous. It's almost as though Jim knows what he's doing... .*

Silver & Sand

Adapted from a recipe by
TJ Vytlacil,
Franco,
Saint Louis, MO.

"Ted Kilgore and I have an obsession with the Blood and Sand cocktail. This is my summer version. I took this drink to the Greater Kansas City Competition and did well with it. Thank you for the consideration."
—TJ Vytlacil.

30 ml (1 oz) Ginger and Lemon Infused Dewar's 12-Year-Old Scotch Whisky*

30 ml (1 oz) Lillet Rouge

30 ml (1 oz) fresh lemon juice

30 ml (1 oz) Cherry Heering

1 egg white

1 lemon twist, as garnish

2 to 3 drops The Bitter Truth Lemon bitters, as garnish

Dry-shake for 15 seconds, then fill with ice. Shake vigorously for 25 seconds and fine-strain into a chilled cocktail glass. Add the garnishes.

*Ginger and Lemon Infused Dewar's 12-Year-Old Scotch Whisky:

Put 3 lemon teabags and 3 ginger teabags into a large jar and pour one 750-ml bottle of Dewar's 12-Year-Old scotch over them. Allow to steep for 2 hours then strain off.

gaz sez: *So this TJ Vytlacil person is a friend of Ted Kilgore's , huh? And if you know Ted Kilgore, you'll know what a crazy bastard he is. And we know that craziness can filter down, right? And craziness*

323

can lead to brilliance, too. Such is the case with this drink.

Don't miss out by not trying Silver & Sand. The infused scotch on its own is worth making. It works very well indeed in a Hot Toddy, for instance, but when you use it in this drink it really springs to life—it marries perfectly with the Lillet Rouge and the Cherry Heering; the lemon juice gives the drink balance, and the egg white provides a velvety texture. This is a fabulous drink.

Smoking Aces

Adapted from a recipe by
Duane Fernandez, Jr., Entwine,
New York City, NY.

"I wanted to create a classic-style cocktail with a fantastic aged tequila... ."
—Duane Fernandez, Jr.

75 ml (2.5 oz) Don Modesto añejo tequila

30 ml (1 oz) pure maple syrup

1 dash liquid smoke

1 lemon twist, as garnish

Stir over ice and strain into a chilled coupe. Flame the lemon twist over the drink, then add as garnish.

gaz sez: *I usually hate maple syrup in cocktails, and although this isn't the only drink that calls for it that I've liked, it's one of a very few. The liquid smoke is the ingredient that compensates for the maple sweetness here, and it adds dimension to the cocktail, too. Nicely done, Duane.*

The Smoking Gun

Adapted from a recipe by
**Lynette Marerro,
Peels**
and
DrinksAt6,
New York City, NY.

Winner of the 2010 Metropolitan Opera Cocktail Competition. Organized by Allen Katz, judged by Allen Katz, Tyne Daly, Susan Graham, and gaz regan.

7.5 ml (.25 oz) Cio Ciaro

52.5 ml (1.75 oz) Rittenhouse rye whiskey

1 teaspoon Smoked Demerara*

1 dash Bittermens Xocolatl Mole bitters

1 dash Angostura bitters

1 orange twist, as garnish

Stir over ice and strain into a rocks glass over ice. Flame the twist over the drink, then add as garnish.

***Smoked Demerara**: Steep 1 tablespoon lapsong souchong tea leaves in 240 ml (1 cup) boiling water for 2 hours. Add tea to 200 g (1 cup) demerara over medium heat. Simmer and reduce. Cool, strain, and bottle.

gaz sez: *I've a sneaking suspicion that Lynette came up with this one with Allen and me in mind—it's right up both of our alleys! Just fabulous. Hanging out with Tyne Daly and Susan Graham wasn't shabby, either!*

Smokin' Orange

Adapted from a recipe by
**Tarcisio Costa,
Alfama**,
New York City, NY.

"For lovers of smoky flavors, this is a great fall/winter cocktail."
—Tarcisio Costa.

1 lemon twist, as garnish

90 ml (3 oz) Combier liqueur d'orange

15 ml (.5 oz) Laphroaig 10 Year Old scotch whisky

15 ml (.5 oz) fresh lemon juice

Rub the yellow part of the lemon twist on the lip of a
chilled whisky tumbler and drop it in; add ice. Set aside.
Shake all ingredients over ice for about 20 and strain
into the glass.

gaz sez: *Simple and pretty stupendous. Nice one,
Tarcisio.*

Speakeasy

Adapted from a recipe by
**Oscar Quagliarini,
Juleps New York Bar**,
Milan, Italy.

"A twist on the Sazerac."
—Oscar Quagliarini.

1 sugar cube

70 ml (2.3 oz) Ardbeg Ten Years Old scotch whisky

1 barspoon Galliano L'Autentico

3 drops The Bitter Truth Old Time Aromatic bitters

3 drops The Bitter Truth Chocolate bitters

Pernod, as rinse

Crush the sugar cube in a mixing glass. Add ice and
the remaining ingredients. Stir and strain into a chilled
Pernod-rinsed old-fashioned glass.

gaz sez: *Here's another brave soul. I'm amazed
that the Ardbeg doesn't drown out the other ingredients here, but they all come into play in very
subtle ways, and I love the way that the scotch and
the Galliano L'Autentico waltz. They're so damned
aggressive, and they're so damned graceful, too.*

Spring Blossom

Adapted from a recipe by
Diana Haider,
EWG Spirits & Wine,
Cognac, France.

"I started bartending about 10 years ago in Berlin. There I worked together with the guys from *Mixology* at the Lore Berlin before they started the magazine. Afterwards I worked in different bars, clubs, and catering companies. Now I'm living in Frankfurt since a few years and I did spend the last two and a half years at a place called Blumen, a very small, lovely restaurant and bar. Recently I stopped working there to open a new bar with another company."
—Diana Haider.

50 ml (1.65 oz) G'Vine Floraison gin

20 ml (.66 oz) Japanese Syrup*

1 barspoon maraschino liqueur

10 ml (.33 oz) L'Esprit de June

30 ml (1 oz) fresh lime juice

Ginger beer

1 cucumber spear, as garnish

1 mint sprig, as garnish

Build in a highball glass over ice. Add the garnishes.

*Japanese Syrup: I tried chrysanthemum and jasmine tea syrup. I just cooked a very strong tea by using a lot of tea bags (I didn't let it soak too long, because I didn't want any bitterness in there) and then I made a simple syrup out of the teas. Both of them worked well in this drink but I liked most both together (1:1), to make it round I added the peels of two limes and I let it steep for about three hours.

329

gaz sez: *This is a very unusual drink—très floral, a little spicy—depending on which ginger beer you use—and très chic. Nicely done, Diana.*

The Standard

Adapted from a recipe by
**Mathias Simonis,
Distil**,
Milwaukee, WI.

"This is a drink I did for the bar and nightclub show in Las Vegas in March 2010. It propelled me into the final five of 32 and I ended up taking third place among a field of amazing talent. This drink has now become my #1 seller at the bar, which in a city like Milwaukee, where vodka-based "tinis" and beer run king and queen, is pretty much saying something. It has been a great tool to get people to trust the

331

bartender to go outside their comfort zone and try other spirit-based cocktails and classics and has done wonders to get the public to try new things."

—Mathias Simonis.

30 ml (1 oz) Plymouth gin

15 ml (.5 oz) Luxardo maraschino liqueur

15 ml (.5 oz) St. Germain

15 ml (.5 oz) fresh lemon juice

1 egg white

5 to 6 drops Fee Brothers Rhubarb bitters

1 lemon twist, as garnish

Dry-shake, then add ice. Hard-shake and double-strain into a chilled coupe. Add the garnish, spraying the oil over the froth before adding to the drink.

gaz sez: *This is a fairly simple drink, but it gets lots of extra points for the dimension that the Fee Brothers Rhubarb bitters brings to this party. The dastardly Joe Fee knows what he's doing when it comes to bitters, and this particular bottling, in my 'umble estimation, really takes the cake.*

Strawberry Blonde

Adapted from a recipe by
**Brad Farran,
Clover Club**,
Brooklyn, NY.

"This drink sealed the deal for me with the people over at StarChefs for the Rising Star 2010 award. I think it's pretty good. Cheers!"
—Brad Farran.

1 strawberry, topped and halved

Fresh cracked pepper

22.5 ml (.75 oz) simple syrup

60 ml (2 oz) Flor de Cana 4 Year-Old Extra Dry white rum

22.5 ml (.75 oz) fresh lemon juice

7.5 ml (.25 oz) egg white

1 barspoon grenadine

1 barspoon white balsamic vinegar

Club soda

Fresh cracked pepper, as garnish

Muddle the strawberry, pepper, and simple syrup in a shaker. Add the remaining ingredients except soda and dry-shake, then add ice. Hard-shake and fine-strain into a highball glass with two ice cubes. Top with club soda and add the garnish.

gaz sez: *This drink is just extraordinary. The combination of strawberry, pepper, and balsamic is simply divine, and it floats down the throat on a raft of rum, grenadine, and lemon juice floating atop a silky egg white. I could go on for years about this one.*

333

Strega's Walnut Manhattan

Adapted from a recipe by
**Victoria D'Amato-Moran,
Cent'Anni Cocktails**,
San Francisco, CA.

1 lemon twist

45 ml (1.5 oz) Old Potrero rye whiskey

15 ml (.5 oz) Carpano Antica Formula vermouth

7.5 ml (.25 oz) plus a dash more Charbay Black Walnut
liqueur

7.5 ml (.25 oz) Strega

Rub the yellow side of the lemon twist over the interior
of a chilled cocktail glass, then discard the twist. Stir the
remaining ingredients over ice and strain the drink into
the prepared glass.

gaz sez: *I've known Victoria for quite a few years, and I've ceased being surprised that her wacky formulas work so well, although the ingredients in this drink aren't quite as strange as those found in some of her other creations.*

For me it's the Charbay Black Walnut liqueur that brings this to life, though I must say that the vanilla notes that the Strega brings to the party give the drink more depth, too. The brilliance in this one, though, lies in the ratio of Old Potrero rye to Carpano Antica Formula vermouth. The Carpano can take charge of a drink if it isn't used judiciously, and Victoria hit the nail on the head when she formulated this one.

Teenage Riot

Adapted from a recipe by
**Tonia Guffey,
Dram,
Flatiron Lounge,**
and **Lani Kai,**
New York City, NY.

45 ml (1.5 oz) Rittenhouse rye whiskey

45 ml (1.5 oz) Cynar

15 ml (.5 oz) Dolin dry vermouth

15 ml (.5 oz) Lustau dry amontillado sherry

2 dashes orange bitters

1 lemon twist, as garnish

Stir over ice and strain into a chilled coupe. Squeeze the
twist over the drink, then add as garnish.

gaz sez: *Tonia wove quite a tapestry when she put this baby together. It's as intricate a drink as you'll find just about anywhere. She didn't specify a brand of orange bitters, so I used a 50/50 mix of Fee Bros and Regans' No. 6, as is common in many bars in the USA. Worked pretty well.*

10 Scotch Cigars

Adapted from a recipe by
**Noah Heaney,
Argyll Gastropub**,
Denver, CO.

"The amount of water introduced by the stir is crucial. Using Kold-Draft I never stir more than 30 seconds. No one likes a diluted cocktail… ."
—Noah Heaney.

45 ml (1.5 oz) Laphroaig 10 Year Old scotch whisky

22.5 ml (.75 oz) Fernet Branca

15 ml (.5 oz) rich demerara simple syrup

1 barspoon verjus blanc

1 orange twist

Stir over ice and strain into a chilled glass. Flame the orange twist over the drink, then discard.

gaz sez: *Okay, here's a weird one. The verjus blanc is an unnecessary ingredient here, in my opinion. It gets completely lost in the mix. On the other hand, Noah is one bloody brave son-of-a-gun to put Laphroaig and Fernet together on the battlefield, and I've got to salute him for not only conceiving of this match, but also for balancing them pretty much perfectly.*

Tessmanian Devil

Adapted from a recipe by
**Tess Posthumus,
Door 74**,
Amsterdam, Netherlands.

"Be careful with the Tabasco and cayenne pepper. Don't make it too spicy, just give it a little spicy aftertaste."
—Tess Posthumus.

20 ml (.66 oz) Beefeater gin

20 ml (.66 oz) Strega

20 ml (.66 oz) Lillet Blanc

20 ml (.66 oz) fresh lemon juice

1 dash Tabasco

1 dash cayenne pepper

1 dash The Bitter Truth Creole bitters

1 piece red chili pepper, as garnish

Shake over ice and fine-strain into a chilled cocktail glass. Add the garnish.

gaz sez: *Tess is right about having to be very careful with the Tabasco and cayenne in the Tessmanian Devil, but if you pull it off and balance this baby well, you'll be making this drink over and over again, I think. Door 74 was the last stop on a very long bar crawl, courtesy the good folk at Bols, in 2010. Hope I didn't misbehave too very badly... .*

Thai Cobbler

Adapted from a recipe by
**Benjamin Tubbs,
Brian's Pourhouse**,
Hood River, OR.

"As some may know, Ty Cobb's nickname was the "Georgia Peach." Well, with the addition of some "Thai" flavors and a play on words as well as on the Whiskey Smash, this is what I've come up with. Please enjoy!"
—Benjamin Tubbs.

339

3 basil leaves (preferably Thai basil)

2 lemon wedges

30 ml (1 oz) fresh peach puree

15 ml (.5 oz) Domaine de Canton ginger liqueur

60 ml (2 oz) Maker's Mark bourbon

1 dash Angostura bitters

1 basil leaf, as garnish

1 peach slice or lemon twist, as garnish

Gently muddle basil and lemon in a mixing glass. Add
ice and the remaining ingredients. Shake and strain into
an old-fashioned glass with fresh ice. Add the garnish.

gaz sez: *Fruity drinks aren't usually to my taste,
but the basil in this one brings the cocktail to a
higher level than most formulas that call for peach
puree and the like. And yes, I added an extra couple of dashes of bitters after tasting the drink, but
I'm a hog for bitters and I reserve my right to go
overboard... .*

30th Century Man

Adapted from a recipe by
**Nathan Weber,
Tavern Law**,
Seattle, WA.

"Named after a Scott Walker song that was featured in the movie *The Life Aquatic*. On the menu at Tavern Law."
—Nathan Weber.

22.5 ml (.75 oz) Ardbeg 10 Years Old scotch whisky

22.5 ml (.75 oz) fresh lemon juice

22.5 ml (.75 oz) Cointreau

22.5 ml (.75 oz) crème de cacao

2 dashes Kübler absinthe

1 brandied cherry, as garnish

Shake over ice and double-strain into a Nick and Nora glass. Add the garnish.

gaz sez: *Get ready for a hall full of hipsters dancing the night away in your throat when you sample this. The drink is all over the place. Be really careful with the absinthe if you make this baby—one dash too many and the whole thing crashes in flames. Something like the Hindenburg. Construct it properly, though, and you've got the Charlie Watts Orchestra Stomping at the Savoy on your tongue.*

Too Soon?

Adapted from a recipe by
**Sam Ross,
Milk & Honey**,
New York City, NY.

"It's a fucking lock for drink of the millennium ;)."
—Sam Ross.

30 ml (1 oz) Beefeater gin

30 ml (1 oz) Cynar

22.5 ml (.75 oz) fresh lemon juice

15 ml (.5 oz) simple syrup

2 orange wedges

Put all to shaker, shake the shit like mad, and strain into
chilled cocktail glass.

gaz sez: <<*It's a fucking lock for drink of the millennium* >> *Fuckin' right it is, Sammy!*

Torch'n Scorch

PART 4 • OTHER PEOPLE'S STUFF

Adapted from a recipe by
Payman Bahmani,
Life's a Cocktail,
Brooklyn, NY.

"For the chipotle sauce, simply blend the entire contents of a can of chipotles en adobo until well pureed and smooth. Hopefully this drink shows that blended drinks, even if not taken seriously, can still be seriously good."
—Payman Bahmani.

60 ml (2 oz) light rum (Banks 5-Island works well)

30 ml (1 oz) cream of coconut

15 ml (.5 oz) fresh lime juice

15 ml (.5 oz) honey

1/2 teaspoon chipotle sauce

10 basil leaves

2 sprigs cilantro (leaves removed from stem)

1 cup crushed ice

1 cherry pepper, as garnish

Place everything in a blender and process on high until smooth. Pour into a margarita glass and add the garnish.

gaz sez: *This is a fabulous drink, and I love the fact that Payman simply threw everything into a blender instead of muddling and shaking and straining, etc. The crowning glory, for me, is the chipotle puree—I dashed to the supermarket to buy a can of chipotles en adobo so I could try this drink, and now I keep chipotle sauce in my fridge at all times—it comes in handy in the kitchen, as well as behind the bar.*

343

Vanilla Skye

Adapted from a recipe by
Adam Brewer,
Cloudland,
Brisbane, Australia.

"This is the winning drink from Australian World Class 2010. I have changed the name to be more suitable. Also the drink is named after the famous Monet painting and the Isle of Skye, from which Talisker hails."
—Adam Brewer.

40 ml (1.33 oz) Talisker 10 Year Old scotch whisky

10 ml (.33 oz) white crème de menthe (the cheaper the better)

10 ml (.33 oz) oloroso sherry

2 dashes chocolate bitters (I use Scrappy's; Bitter Truth or Fee Brothers also work)

1 lemon twist

Stir over ice and strain into a chilled coupette. Garnish with the oils from the lemon then discard the twist.

gaz sez: *I do love the combination of the Talisker, mint, and sherry in this drink. An odd threesome, it's true, but the mint and the sherry tease the scotch nicely.*

The Violent Bear

Adapted from a recipe by
**Jeremy Swift,
The JakeWalk**,
Brooklyn, NY.

"This is a serious drink for before dinner to open the appetite or for after to settle the tummy. Don't let the Violent Bear scare you; in the end it's really well balanced."
—Jeremy Swift.

60 ml (2 oz) Bols Genever

15 ml (.5 oz) Punt e Mes

15 ml (.5 oz) Zirbenz

2 dashes Bittermens Xocolatl Mole bitters

Stir over ice and strain into a chilled coupe.

gaz sez: *Not many people can work well with Zirbenz Stone Pine Liqueur, but Jeremy pulls it off beautifully in the Violent Bear. The combination of the Bols Genever and the Punt e Mes works as a wall that simply blocks the Zirbenz from dominating the drink, but nevertheless, they let it stand up and be counted. This is a very well thought-out drink.*

Virgin de Guadalupe

Adapted from a recipe by
Adrian Biggs,
La Descarga,
Los Angeles, CA.

"Refreshing, light, and delicious. I love the Paloma cocktail, which was my inspiration for creating this libation. Cheers!"
—Adrian Biggs.

45 ml (1.5 oz) blanco tequila

15 ml (.5 oz) yellow Chartreuse

15 ml (.5 oz) fresh lime juice

30 ml (1 oz) fresh grapefruit juice

90 ml (3 oz) ginger beer (preferably spicy and slightly sweet)

1 long grapefruit twist, as garnish

Build in highball glass. Top with ginger beer. Squeeze the twist over the drink, then add as garnish.

gaz sez: *The Chartreuse brings a complexity to this baby, and she plays well with the tequila, too. Adrian didn't push the envelope to come up with this one, but he sure as hell nailed the ingredients and the proportions.*

Visionary

Adapted from a recipe by
**Roman Milostivy,
The United Bartenders**,
Moscow.

40 ml (1.33 oz) vodka

10 ml (.33 oz) Fernet Branca

10 ml (.33 oz) Chamomile & Cinnamon Syrup*

20 ml (.66 oz) fresh lime juice

20 ml (.66 oz) egg white

2 drops chocolate bitters , as garnish

Dry-shake, then add ice. Hard-shake and strain into a
chilled cocktail glass. Drop the bitters on the top. Enjoy!

*Chamomile & Cinnamon Syrup:

Infuse some 3 to 5 chamomile teabags in 1 L of hot but
not boiling water for about 5 to 7 minutes, to get a rich
taste of it. Discard the teabags. Add 600 g (3 cups) of
white caster sugar (you can use brown sugar too for
extra aroma) and dissolve the sugar by stirring the syrup
over low heat. Add approximately 10 cinnamon sticks
(crushed to smaller pieces) and let sit in the syrup on
low heat for 45 to 60 minutes. Do not let it boil. Let the
syrup cool down and strain it through the smallest filter
(can use coffee paper filter) into bottles. Ready to use!

gaz sez: *This syrup is just gorgeous, and it plays
very nicely indeed with the Fernet. The aromatic
garnish seals the deal. Nice drink, Roman.*

Voiron Gold

Adapted from a recipe by
**Merlin Jerebine,
1806**,
Melbourne, Australia.

"My two top loves in the alcohol world are tequila and Chartreuse. I created this one while drinking a Last Word and brainstorming on a Chartreuse list for 1806. I serve this drink to customers who tell me they hate Chartreuse or tequila without letting them know what's in it, and I've had a 99 percent success rate. Depending on the limes, this may need a touch more Frangelico to balance. Cheers."
—Merlin Jerebine.

20 ml (.66 oz) yellow Chartreuse

20 ml (.66 oz) Gran Centenario Tequila Plata

15 ml (.5 oz) Frangelico

20 ml (.66 oz) fresh lime juice

Shake over ice and double-strain into a chilled champagne saucer.

gaz sez: *I love the way that tequila plays nice with Chartreuse, and I put them together in a drink called Mink Coat and No Manners using Don Julio Blanco, green Chartreuse, and a pinch of cayenne pepper. The Voiron Gold goes a step further and the Frangelico adds a fabulous nutty veil to the drink. I also like the way in which Merlin notes that the ratios can vary depending on the acidity of the lime juice.*

I should also mention that Merlin has two recipes in this chapter, and that was not my intention. One drink per bartender was the rule I set down for myself. That said, though, by the time I discovered this faux pas it was too late in the editing/production process to do anything about it. C'est la vie!

Wet Grave

Adapted from a recipe by
**Darcy O'Neil,
Art of Drink**,
London, Ontario, Canada.

"Named after a very old nickname for New Orleans (1820s) and as a tip of the hat to classic cocktails from the 1800s such as the Tombstone and Corpse Reviver."

—Darcy O'Neil.

37.5 ml (1.25 oz) bourbon

15 ml (.5 oz) Claret Syrup*

2 teaspoons dry vermouth

1 teaspoon acid phosphate**

3 dashes Peychaud's bitters

Stir over ice and strain into a chilled cocktail glass.

*__Claret Syrup__: Combine equal parts simple syrup (2:1) and Bordeaux or other red wine.

**For an article on acid phosphate and links to suppliers, go to www.artofdrink.com/ap.

gaz sez: *Darcy is one of the backbones of the cocktail industry in the USA, and he has been for years. He's innovative, creative, and he's constantly moving forward. This drink's a doozy, the acid phosphate adds a note that's almost indescribable, and the claret syrup is a stroke of genius.*

353

The Williamsburg

Adapted from a recipe by
**Clif Travers,
Bar Celona**,
Brooklyn, NY.

"I crossed the Greenpoint with the Red Hook (location, location) and changed the rye to bourbon in a nod to the Williamsburg hipster culture."
—Clif Travers.

7.5 ml (.75 oz) yellow Chartreuse

7.5 ml (.75 oz) Dolin dry vermouth

7.5 ml (.75 oz) Punt e Mes

75 ml (2.5 oz) W.L. Weller bourbon

1 orange twist, as garnish

Stir over ice and strain into a chilled coupe. Add the garnish.

gaz sez: *This one started me looking for the Greenpoint and Red Hook recipes so I could compare, and that led to me finding a slew of other cocktails named for various locations around New York, so I've been all over the web stealing recipes, mainly from Robert Simonson of The New York Times, and updating my personal recipe book. It was a job that had to be done. The good news was that, since all these drinks are basically riffs on the Manhattan, they're right up my alley. And so is the Williamsburg. Nice to see the Weller bourbon cropping up here, too. Great bottling.*

MAKING GOOD DRINKS
IS NOT ENOUGH

"Hopefully [the next big trend will be] hospitality. Giving a shit about what you do. Making good drinks is not enough. Being very perceptive of your guests' experience at your bar, THAT is the important thing. And I think that's coming back."

Jason Littrell, Dram and Death & Co.,
New York.
Source: wweek.com, October 23, 2010,
article by Ruth Brown.

INDEX

A

B

C

grenadine 101, 333
Grey Goose vodka 285
Gruet Blanc de Noirs 296
guests 58, 61, 63, 66, 67, 71, 72, 96, 118, 128, 150, 160, 163, 164, 170, 174, 355

H

Hacienda de Chihuahua Sotol Plata 239
hard shake 110
Havana Club: Añejo 3 Años rum 304; Seleccion rum 277
Hawthorne strainer 119, 120, 130
Hayman's Old Tom gin 242
Hendrick's gin 263, 298
Hennessy VS cognac 258
Hess, Robert 118, 145
Hess' House Bitters 145
Hey, Stephen "Hoss" 39, 50
highball 97, 100, 227, 263, 299, 307, 329, 333, 347
Hoerth, Maxime 130
Horse and Jockey 23, 24, 25, 27
hour of hush and wonder 64
Hulme, Pam 39, 51

I

ice 68, 79, 94, 95, 100, 104, 106, 107, 109, 110, 111, 112, 113, 114, 115,
117, 118, 120, 122, 129, 130, 182, 191, 192, 194, 195, 201, 204, 206,
208, 209, 212, 213, 214, 216, 218, 220, 221, 223, 224, 225, 227, 228,
230, 233, 234, 235, 236, 237, 239, 240, 244, 245, 247, 249, 251, 252,
254, 255, 256, 257, 258, 259, 261, 262, 263, 266, 268, 269, 270, 271,
273, 274, 275, 278, 279, 281, 282, 283, 285, 287, 288, 289, 290, 291,
292, 293, 295, 296, 297, 298, 299, 300, 303, 304, 306, 307, 308, 310,
311, 313, 314, 317, 318, 320, 322, 323, 325, 326, 327, 328, 329, 332,
333, 335, 336, 337, 338, 340, 341, 343, 344, 346, 349, 350, 353, 354;
crushed 94, 95, 113, 244, 299, 306, 343
ingredients 54, 78, 79, 80, 81, 82, 92, 93, 95, 96, 97, 98, 100, 101, 102, 103,
104, 105, 106, 109, 115, 117, 118, 122, 128, 129, 136, 141, 142, 144,
145, 180, 183, 184, 191, 194, 195, 198, 199, 200, 201, 206, 208, 209,
210, 214, 218, 219, 220, 221, 224, 230, 231, 236, 240, 244, 245, 249,
250, 251, 253, 255, 256, 258, 261, 263, 269, 270, 272, 274, 275, 280,
282, 285, 287, 288, 291, 295, 296, 298, 299, 304, 306, 310, 311, 313,
325, 327, 328, 333, 335, 337, 340, 347
Institute for Mindful Living, The 73
intuition 58, 59, 60, 61, 72, 78, 79, 80, 97
Irvin, Barry 28

J

Jacko Diamonds 43, 45
Jackson, Angie 80, 271

361

M

N

S

W

X

Y

Z